CONSTAB

The Rise of Police Institutions in Britain, the Commonwealth and the United States

*Dedicated to Professor Charles Bayley,
who has been a constant inspiration
throughout my academic career.*

CONSTABULARY

The Rise of Police Institutions in Britain, the Commonwealth and the United States

HEREWARD SENIOR

Dundurn Press
Toronto • Oxford

Editor: Nigel Wood
Designer: Sebastian Vasile
Printer: Best Book Manufacturers

Canadian Cataloguing in Publication Data

Senior, Hereward
    Constabulary: the rise of police institutions in Britain, the Commonwealth and the
    United States

Includes bibliographical references and index.
ISBN 1-55002-246-6

1. Police – Great Britain – History.   2. Police – Commonwealth countries – History.
3. Police – United States – History.   I. Title.

HV7903. S46 1997   363.2'09   C96-932588-6

1   2   3   4   5   NW   01   00   99   98   97

The publisher wishes to acknowledge the generous assistance of the **Canada Council,** the **Book Publishing Industry Development Program** of the **Department of Canadian Heritage,** and the **Ontario Arts Council.**

Care has been taken to trace the ownership of copyright material used in this book. The author and the publisher welcome any information enabling them to rectify any references or credit in subsequent editions.

Printed and bound in Canada.

Printed on recycled paper.

Dundurn Press
2181 Queen Street East
Suite 301
Toronto, Ontario, Canada
M4E 1E5

Dundurn Press
73 Lime Walk
Headington, Oxford
England
OX3 7AD

Dundurn Press
250 Sonwil Drive
Buffalo, NY
U.S.A. 14225

CONTENTS

PREFACE

THIS BOOK IS BASED ON a series of lectures dealing with police institutions which I began twenty years ago. It then attracted 16 students: last year's enrolment was ninety. As there existed no suitable text for the course, my lecture notes soon became the basis of one. Since I had other writing obligations, some years elapsed before I could turn these notes into a manuscript suitable for publication. As it stands now I hope it may prove a useful aid to those engaged in police work, including those employed by private security agencies, as well as be of interest to the general public.

In my lectures I attempted to explain the origins of common law and the problem it presented to law enforcement. There existed for centuries well-founded doubts about the compatibility of professional police with common law. In the course of these lectures I also endeavoured to explain how, by degrees, these doubts were overcome, with the resulting emergence of imperfect but reasonably efficient professional forces operating in different areas of the world with common law jurisdictions. No effort was or is made to provide a comprehensive treatment of all such forces, but in tracing the history of several of the largest, representative of others, the intention remains to sketch how they came into being and developed.

In preparing this study my principal coadjutor has been Bruce Dolphin, of the McGill University Archives, who struggled with my handwriting and put the text into word-processor form. Nigel Wood, of Dundurn Press, was also of great assistance, as was the staff of the Notman Photographic Archives at the McCord Museum of Canadian History. My thanks to Garry Toffoli for providing the photograph used on page 175 and the two colour photographs used on the cover, and to Claudia Willetts for making the index. I also wish to thank Prof. David Mulhall, of Montreal's Dawson College, a former Bermuda policeman, and Fred Gaffen, of the Canadian War Museum, who have enlivened my course with fascinating guest lectures. Finally, I owe a debt to my graduate student, and for the last two years my teaching assistant in the police course, Marc Drolet.

CHAPTER I

ORIGIN OF COMMON LAW POLICE: ANGLO-SAXONS TO 18TH CENTURY

THIS VOLUME IS AN EFFORT to trace the origins and major developments of police institutions under the common law jurisdiction broadly shared by Great Britain and those parts of the globe significantly influenced by the British Empire and its constitutional-legal heritage. Therefore, while England is the point of departure, Ireland, Canada, the United States, Australia, India and South Africa are also featured. Common law's perhaps most readily recognized feature is the presumption of innocence: the burden of proof rests on the accuser. Other long established key components are *habeas corpus* and further protections against arbitrary search and seizure; freedom of speech, association and assembly; and trial by jury. Such principles superintend and inform the common law system, but it is rather with its human agents — or rather one particular set of them, the police, not judges nor lawyers nor other officers of the court — that this study is mainly concerned.

Common law places restraints on the exercise of police power not found in most societies, though some element of the police function is present in any community. Primitive societies, having little division of labour, are as a rule self-policing, with the enforcement of standards of approved behaviour vested virtually in the whole community. As the division of labour develops, the police function is increasingly provided by amateur, unpaid individuals in rudimentary organizations. But it is only with the coming of civilization and its highly sophisticated divisions of labour that professional police forces can make their appearance.

In Anglo-American society the latest stage of law enforcement came late, indeed when it was long over due. For this a price was paid in crime waves, civil disorder and human suffering, but the end achievement was the creation of police forces in the common law tradition dedicated to the idea of public service rather than public domination, the first professionals on the scene in this connection being the London Metropolitan Police in 1829. This force provided a model, never perfectly reproduced, not only for urban police in most parts of the world where English common law prevailed, but for the more peaceful of their rural areas as well. The unsuitability of this example for frontier societies or for otherwise chronically disturbed rural areas, however, led to the adoption in such cases of a different approach. There, the model turned out to be the Royal Irish Constabulary which (at first known simply as the Irish Constabulary) emerged in Ireland in 1836, seven years after the advent of the London Metropolitan Police.

Professional police appear in ancient times, reaching a kind of peak in the early centuries of the Roman Empire. Yet they and their predecessors, as far as can be determined, thought of themselves as agents of state power and control rather than servants of their fellow citizens or society in the wider sense. The English experience was unique, made possible by the insular character of Britain which enabled its inhabitants to accept handicaps which would have ruined any of the contemporary Continental states. England in due course shared this privilege with the American Colonies, protected as they were by isolation and sea power. In consequence, Britain could fight a civil war without external intervention in the seventeenth century, just as the Americans did in the nineteenth century. Societies less favorably endowed geographically found that their domestic quarrels often brought opportunistic foreign intervention.

As nothing save roads and Celtic fragments of Christianity seems to have survived the Roman occupation of Britain, English law is in its origin Germanic. Before the appearance of written law there existed in German culture an official called a "law speaker" who memorized the entire criminal and civil codes. Law speakers survived until the tenth century in parts of Ireland, but appear to have vanished in England after St. Augustine landed in Kent in 597. The Anglo-Saxons in any case brought to England German tribal custom, preserved by oral tradition and enforced by society as a whole. Tribal customs survived the crossing of the North Sea, but tribal identities were less enduring. The Saxon colonists who after a century or two conquered Roman Britain seem to have come as ship companies rather than extended families. In their new environment they preserved the sub-division known as the hundred. Originally a hundred families or perhaps a hundred warriors, in England it became a territorial division. The hundred, presided over by a headman or reeve, held court every thirty days, when all freemen assembled to settle local affairs.

In the late Saxon period the hundreds were divided into tythings or groups of ten men responsible for one another's conduct, and bound to present for trial at the hundred court any offender within their group. One of the tything's number would be designated the spokesman for the group, such spokesman sometimes being referred to as the headborough. This minor official seems to be the ultimate ancestor of the parish constable who became the chief police officer in the later middle ages and indeed survived well into the nineteenth century.

The hundred was a rural territorial division which even in early Saxon times included some boroughs which were, in theory at least, urban inasmuch as they had a charter from the king establishing them as legal entities. Many boroughs were soon to acquire equal status with the hundred and with it separate representation at the shire or county court. Larger boroughs, like London designated cities, went further, acquiring equal status with the shire or county while they enjoyed a direct link with the crown completely separate from the shire.

The emergence of the shire appears to be the result of the consolidation of the small Saxon states into regional kingdoms of which there existed seven when England re-entered written history with the arrival of St. Augustine in Kent near the end of the sixth century A.D. The shire court was organized by the king's man in the shire, the shire-reeve (later the sheriff), who nevertheless did not preside over the court. The latter role fell to a regional noble-man, the ealdorman, who might in fact preside at more than one shire court. There would also be a bishop present to handle cases which touched on church law such as the discipline of the clergy, and probate which dealt with wills and inheritances.

Sheriffs constitute the first police officers in English history, but even so they served only in a part-time capacity, charged with seeing to the peace and good order of the king's personal property or royal domain within each shire. The Saxon sheriff is therefore a distant ancestor of the sheriff in the nineteenth century American west, in that he pursued law-breakers assisted by a *posse comita-tus* (a temporary law-enforcement body) put together for the occa-sion, and his authority likewise ceased at the county line.

The regional kingdoms were swept away by the invasion of the Danes, but the latter were in turn eventually contained and incorporated into a single kingdom by Alfred the Great who died in 899. For the next several centuries, until the imposition of the Norman hegemony, there existed one English kingdom but three systems of law: the law of Wessex (Alfred's original kingdom); the law of Mercia (roughly the midlands); and Danelaw, each develop-ing its own precedents as in common law. That is to say they fea-tured parallel but separate legal regimes growing by precedent, the precedents being independent of one another.

In theory the Norman Conquest was not a conquest at all, for even after his hard-won victory over King Harold at Hastings in 1066, William of Normandy followed English law by consenting to election by the witan (the council of notables periodically called to advise the king), and then further confirming his assumption of the crown by the formality of a coronation. In practice, however, exten-sive legal changes ensued although these took time. Separate church courts were established, the process of inquest which con-tained the germ of trial by jury was introduced, and itinerant justices toured the shires, now called counties, bringing England under a single system of law. Also, by degrees French, the language of the Norman ruling classes, became the language of the courts.

Inquest began with the *Domesday Book* in 1085, when what was in effect a royal commission toured England, calling local witnesses to attest to the extent of their neighbourhood's wealth and property ownership. In 1166, a hundred years after the conquest, an assembly of notables at the Assize of Clarendon (an assize being literally a sitting, in Norman French) regularized and made it the standard procedure to send out itinerant justices (justices-in-eyre) to the counties. At the same time they established the universal practice of local residents forming juries of presentment (grand juries) to present the accused for trial by the itinerant justices.

These juries of presentment possessed the competence to declare facts but not law, and as accusers they could not decide the question of guilt or innocence. This was left to the more primitive methods of trial by ordeal, trial by combat, or the process of compurgation by which witnesses would under oath testify to the character of the plaintiff or accused but not directly on the question of guilt or innocence. Petty juries which decided guilt or innocence came into existence after 1217 when the Lateran Council of the church condemned trial by ordeal and combat as un-Christian. Such petty juries were created by borrowing jurors from juries of presentment. As there were many of these assembled at county courts, it proved possible to assemble twelve men from them to deal with cases in which they had not been involved in the accusing or presenting of the particular person to be tried.

About 1190 a new county officer appears on the scene to deal with cases in which the crown held a special interest: the crowner, or coroner. Such cases encompassed matters as disparate as the discovery of treasure, the disposal of royal fish (which anomalously included whales — sea-going mammals, not fish — found on the beach), and death under unusual circumstances. The coroner in the performance of his duty assembled a jury whose purpose was inquest: in other words, to discover whether a crime had been committed. The question of by whom rested with a jury of presentment, and guilt or innocence with a petty jury.

As the system of law evolved, so did the system of law enforcement, but this mostly involved changes in name. The sheriff, in charge of prisoners, remained the chief police officer in the county, authorized to when necessary raise a *posse comitatus* to assist in law enforcement. Apart from having responsibility for elections and the selection of juries, the sheriff also served as the chief military officer of the county until the appearance of the lord lieutenant in Tudor times. The reeve of the hundred in some cases became the high constable, while the headborough in most instances assumed the duties and name of parish constable. Matters were further complicated by the emergence of manorial courts which possessed limited jurisdiction on manorial territory, the latter often being an assemblage of non-contiguous properties. Control of hundred courts easily drifted into the hands of local noblemen who thereby acquired the ability to exercise authority in the king's name. *De facto* judicial and police power usually resided with barons who might exercise it either in a private capacity or by control of the local agencies of royal justice. Indeed the *Magna Carta* of 1215, ultimately a document of great constitutional importance in the history of personal liberty, retarded the development of police institutions by strengthening baronial power relative to that of the crown.

Apart from this there existed the boroughs and cities. Divided into wards, these sometimes, as in the case of London, elected their sheriffs. An alderman, whose position was much like a reeve, headed each ward, and assemblies of aldermen headed by a mayor ran borough affairs. Since there obtained no uniform system of election or selection, it is difficult to generalize about the office of alderman or mayor, but for police matters the cities and boroughs had a dimension not present in counties and hundreds: they maintained a force of watchmen. The watchmen, however, were an indifferent lot, recruited in most part from the elderly, the infirm or the otherwise unemployable, with no power of arrest. When patrolling the streets at night an alderman, and later a magistrate, possessed of such power often accompanied them. The watchmen's function, even in theory, never amounted to more than raising hue and cry to enable the citizenry to take action against criminals.

In mediaeval England woodlands and some varieties of wildlife enjoyed better protection than most human beings. Where the Saxon wood reeve had regulated life in the forest, after the Norman Conquest authority long resided in the hands of the sheriff who as the king's agent protected vert and venison. Deer and wild boar could legally be hunted only by the monarch or those designated by him, while lesser animals might be pursued by the inhabitants under certain conditions. "Nuisance" species such as the fox and the wild cat benefitted from no protection. Each royal forest had a special officer appointed as its particular protector, variously a sheriff, warden, master forester, or bailiff, which office became hereditary in feudal England, and in such case profitable. Under them served the steward who patrolled the forest, with the legal right to arrest. Below the steward, in turn, ranked the verderers, and finally the forest constable, both also with the power of arrest.

Special courts sat every week to deal with petty breaches of forest law, serious offences being tried by the forest court or eyre which met only once every year. Punishment could be harsh, including maiming, blinding or other mutilation, and even death; but the infrequency of court meetings made it difficult to get convictions. The forest eyre was later replaced by the swainmote which handled both petty and serious offences. This body, staffed by a vereederer appointed by the crown and six elected verderers, like its predecessors functioned under the limitations of trial by jury. As the legend of Robin Hood reveals, forest laws and courts were unpopular, yet they had the positive function of protecting wildlife and woodlands which would otherwise have been eradicated by the rural human population.

In Saxon and early Norman times the traditional tribal division of chief, elders, and tribal assembly had no counterpart at the top of society, as the witan and the later Norman *curia regius* were essentially a council of elders or a "house of lords," but a measure of popular representation survived at the county level in the county courts, as all freemen were in theory present to deal with general civic administration as well as justice. In the 1300s a significant start toward increased popular, or at least a wider, input into the determination of matters of national concern appeared when the commons — that is the knights representing the counties, and burgesses representing the boroughs — who had only occasionally been summoned by the sovereign in the previous century, began to meet more regularly with the other components of parliament (i.e., the king and the lords). With parliament addressing national issues, and the parish constable attending to his local duties, at the intermediate level of the county the official first designated conservator of the peace came on the scene at the turn of the fourteenth century, a development which signalled a shift of local power from the baronial class to the gentry. By 1327 justice of the peace was already replacing conservator of the peace as the established name; by 1360 the office had absorbed most of the functions of the sheriff who nonetheless still managed county elections, selected juries, presided over executions and appointed agents to seize property for debt. However, the general movement of local police matters was into the hands of two categories of unpaid amateurs, the aforementioned justice of the peace and the parish constable.

Commissions of the peace, the authorization granted by the privy council in the king's name to individuals to serve as justices of the peace (later commonly also called magistrates), carried with them considerable prestige, and consequently proved attractive to local squires who aspired to importance. Justices of the peace met four times a year in quarter sessions, where they handled most of the county's business and tried minor crimes, though the more important cases remained the preserve of a circuit judge sent out from the central Courts of King's Bench or Common Pleas. On the other hand the office of parish constable involved responsibilities without rewards or, in some cases, any apparent pressing need; it accordingly came to be viewed as an imposition something like compulsory military service in peacetime. The position of constable, although in theory elected, was in practice usually foisted upon a parish member required to serve for a year, with luck no more than once in a lifetime. The parish constable, under the supervision of the justice of the peace, held responsibility for such things as the maintenance of roads, the enforcement of whatever sanitary regulations existed, and other mundane parish obligations. He also commanded the power of arrest but could not easily exercise it without jeopardizing his popularity in the community. Parish constables varied widely in the enthusiasm and efficiency with which they performed their duties, and some doubtless became standing jokes, as suggested by the characters Dogberry and Verges in Shakespeare's comedy *Much Ado About Nothing*.

Law and order broke down during the Wars of the Roses (1451-1485), leaving what police function as existed in the control of the warring factions of the feudal nobility. During this temporary resurgence of baronial power local military magnates packed juries and determined that sheriffs, justices of the peace and

Early London watchmen. Above is a watchman from the reign of Elizabeth I. Below (left) are two from the early seventeenth century, each equipped with lantern, pike and bell. Below (right) is a watchman from the reign of James I. Evidence of the position's declining powers can be seen in the fact that the pike has now been replaced by a staff.

constables served regional strongmen rather than the royal or the common interest. However, the coming of the victorious Tudors after more than a generation of dynastic civil war brought about a civilianization of the previously turbulent aristocracy, with castles giving way to unfortified country houses and private armies of retainers disappearing as a matter of royal policy. In future, in time of external war or internal rebellion the crown had to raise temporary forces which often included foreign mercenaries. For while the nobility and gentry still frequently showed an amateur interest in the profession of arms, only those who went on active service in behalf of England or foreign powers became professional.

Police power in Tudor and Stuart times rested firmly in the hands of the justice of the peace and the parish constable, who could henceforth usually exercise it without much fear of external interference. This condition changed little even during the Reformation in spite of some popular tumults and the attempted Catholic uprising in 1536 known as the Pilgrimage of Grace. There existed no standing army, and although the theoretical obligation of all able-bodied freemen to serve in the militia remained, in reality the militia consisted of little more than a handful of trained bands of which the most conspicuous survivor is the City of London's Honourable Artillery Company. Command of the county militia passed during the reign of Queen Mary (1547-1558) from the sheriff to a new officer, the lord lieutenant of the county, a position of some social and political distinction though little in the way of military power. Justices of the peace were normally appointed on the advice of the lord lieutenant, but the latter exercised no formal authority over them and remained in most cases merely a first among equals.

Since England was a country of villages, most of these small, and population movement minimal by later standards, the justice of the peace and parish constable dealt with people they knew personally. Under these conditions of intimacy law enforcement remained relatively simple. A village containing about six hundred persons who lived in perhaps sixty households. Local affairs came under the management of a church warden assisted by vestry meetings which were in effect a village council. One of the greatest chronic problems which arose was that of dealing with vagrants who under the Elizabethan Poor Law were to be returned to their original villages where the home parish was responsible for their welfare. Getting relief was difficult as laws could force the able-bodied to work as domestic servants or farm labourers.

This justice of the peace and parish constable system survived in some rural areas down to the nineteenth century, but a radical interruption occurred as a result of the Civil War of the 1640s. After the eventual defeat of King Charles I's forces, England became subject to what amounted to an internal conquest. The victorious Puritan army vanquished its erstwhile Scottish Presbyterian allies, seized and executed the king, and purged parliament. These same Puritan forces also made their commander, Oliver Cromwell, the Lord Protector (which amounted to military dictator), and imposed their own extremely austere version of Protestant morality on what was culturally still Shakespeare's England. The theatre, Sunday games and travel, the celebration of Easter and Christmas, and the pursuit of most forms of artistic endeavour, were amongst the many activities discouraged or proscribed outright as being too Catholic or otherwise impure. An army of thirty thousand disciplined men enforced a narrow, rigorous brand of law and order, and in the course of so doing gave the country the most extensive police protection it was ever to experience. England was divided into eleven military districts, each under the control of a major-general in command of about twelve hundred soldiers, mostly cavalry, who made the streets safe by constant patrol and enforced curfew at night.

This constituted the first case of clearly visible minority rule since the Norman Conquest, on this occasion the conquest being the work of a minority religious group (about twenty per cent of the kingdom, represented originally by about fifty members of parliament). Cromwell claimed to believe in government by consent but, as he asked, "Where is such consent to be found?" The vitality of the increasingly unpopular regime depended on the genius of Cromwell himself, and it collapsed of its own weight within two years of his death in 1658. There existed an obvious alternative to Puritan domination in the person of the exiled King Charles II, who reclaimed the throne in 1660. The monarchy, and with it the power of the justice of the peace and the parish constables, was restored, but the habits which sustained the old police system had in part been eroded. In particular, those elected or appointed constables more frequently evaded what they deemed the unreasonable responsibilities imposed on them, by hiring substitutes. The substitutes, in turn, often simply neglected to work for their money. In small villages things could still go on as before, but even there the plague which swept Britain in 1666 required a special "plague watch" to keep persons from infected areas. Most towns began to maintain a rudimentary night watch which was perhaps better than nothing, but because of highwaymen the roads between towns were increasingly no longer safe by day or night.

Fear of police power, increased by the Cromwellian experience, ensured the survival of the mediaeval system. The result meant living with an ever-increasing incidence of crime which England endured for another century and a half. In this the larger cities, above all the capital, suffered the most. The level of law and order remained low nationally, but in London the situation became close to being unbearable even by the relaxed standards of the day, seemingly leaving the city at the mercy of a growing, predatory underworld which the constable and justice of the peace could not control. The number of offences which could carry the death penalty had increased, though for the most part gradually, since at least the reign of Henry II in the twelfth century. These, especially those involving crimes against property, now began to greatly proliferate haphazardly as a reaction to the rising lawlessness of the times, reaching a total of at least two hundred by the late eighteenth century.

The argument that an executed felon could not commit another crime possessed an undeniable logic, though the extent to which execution or lesser harsh punishments such as transportation acted as a deterrent is a moot point. One factor, for instance, which came into play was the frequent reluctance of juries to convict obviously guilty parties whom they nonetheless considered did not warrant a possible capital sentence for the non-violent theft of as little as five shillings. And, by the same token, while many judges reflected the brutality and coarseness of the age, like all men they varied in conscience and temperament; hence numbers of them showed sufficient human understanding and compassion to pass much less than the maximum sentence. Moreover, as the criminal statute book grew in piecemeal confusion so did the likelihood that the accused, however guilty in fact, could escape conviction in law by means of a technicality. Effective justice was in retreat and, as the humanitarian and legal reformer Sir Samuel Romilly noted, for the accused the judicial process came to resemble a lottery. Plainly the law as it existed remained inadequate, as did the police instruments which served it and therefore society.

The original City of London (as distinct from the subsequent colloquial, collective term "city of London" or simply "London") was, and still is, a legal entity of about one square mile, with its own lord mayor and police force. But by 1700 it was already only part of a greater more or less urbanized area of contiguous parishes, which spread into several counties and is now known as Metropolitan London. The City in the early eighteenth century was divided into twenty-six wards, each presided over by an alderman who held the authority of a magistrate and, once elected, could subject to good behaviour hold office for life. Aldermen in turn chose the lord mayor, whose powers were shared by an elected common council of over two hundred, each member having a one year term. One constable officially served each of the twenty-six each wards and seldom independently attempted to exercise authority beyond its boundaries, though legally he could do so. To coordinate police authority the board of aldermen appointed a marshal and six marshal men.

Each ward possessed its own night watch, each member being paid from £13 to £20 per annum; but unlike the constable they exercised no power of arrest and in any case drew their recruits from among the old and incapable. In the eighteenth century they numbered seven hundred and thirty-six, bearing the sobriquet "Charlies" as a momento of their organization in the reign of Charles I. But even this inadequate force found no counterpart outside the City walls, leaving much of what is now Metropolitan London under rural government, i.e. the unpaid magistrates and unpaid constables, as there was no marshal and no watch.

This all but total police vacuum was filled partly by what became known as trading magistrates, and partly by bounty hunters who styled themselves thief-takers. The conviction of a highwayman brought a thief-taker a reward of £40; lesser offences received smaller compensation. Trading magistrates meanwhile sold justice by such devices as arresting minor offenders and collecting bail in full knowledge that the offender would not appear in court. Constables rarely performed their functions, and thief-takers preferred to arrest beginners in crime, sometimes after having first induced juveniles to commit offences so that they could be apprehended and the reward collected.

London benefitted from no protection against organized crime, and very little against the casual variety. Much of the population regarded the "right to riot" as a civil liberty, and the only means of controlling such disorders remained resort to the military. Under the Riot Act of 1714, troops could be called out in aid of the civil power by a magistrate. When invoking the Riot Act the procedure consisted of the magistrate publicly reading an order for the crowd to disperse in the name of the sovereign and, upon this being ignored or otherwise defied, the officer in charge of the troops could order them to fire on those now illegally assembled, whatever other offences they might or might not be committing. Soldiers taking action before the Riot Act was duly promulgated were individually liable to prosecution for such serious crimes as murder, attempted murder or assault, however, and magistrates reading the act incurred great personal risk as they faced reprisal from the crowd after the troops departed.

Given the absence of effective justice, it is not surprising that the underworld took steps to take over the police function. The most spectacular effort to do so was made by Jonathan Wild (1682-1725), who left his wife and young son behind in his native Wolverhampton, while he went to London and for a time pursued his original lawful employment as a buckle-maker. Arrested thereafter for debt, his term of imprisonment turned out to be an education in the ways of an underworld he came to substantially dominate.

Wild, being at first without friends in London, began at the bottom but, as stated, found prison to be a profitable school of crime. Seeing little advantage in the risks of being an ordinary thief himself, after his release he at one and the same time set up as a receiver of stolen goods and a thief-taker. Working both sides of the law, he organized an extensive network of criminals and regularly dealt with miscreants committing robberies, paying the thieves a minimal sum for the stolen goods, and then contacting the victims to arrange return of their property for a much higher price. As Wild with his gang and contacts also learned the identities of the authors of a wide range of other crimes, independent criminals were arrested by him for the bounty in his capacity as thief-taker. He vaingloriously styled himself the "thief-taker-general" and at the height of his career owned, besides other property, warehouses and a ship. But in the end Wild's recklessness over-reached itself. He made too many enemies in both respectable society and the underworld, and in time the law worked his undoing. The thief-taker-general finally went to the gallows at Tyburn where he had sent so many others, convicted of criminally restoring to its owner ten guineas worth of stolen lace after first being acquitted of stealing it.

Such scandalous proceedings made it evident that something must be done, and as local government was powerless responsibility came to rest with the secretary of state. Thus at the highest levels of government there soon began a clandestine subsidization of law enforcement which generations later ultimately gave the home office the open, acknowledged control of the London Metropolitan Police.

The first gesture toward introducing professionalism into police work came in 1729 with the appointment of Thomas de Veil (1684-1747) to the commission of the peace for the county of Middlesex and city of Westminster. De Veil, the son of a poor clergyman of Huguenot background, joined the army in the ranks, won promotion to captain, and then found himself placed on half-pay. He might have remained just another trading magistrate like the rest, but he chose for the most part to actually enforce the law. From the beginning he challenged the underworld, initially with more or less futile efforts to check the illegal manufacture and sale of gin; but subsequently, with much more success, by breaking up criminal gangs. De Veil did this at the risk of his life, and showed no hesitation in petitioning the secretary of state for financial support. Since public opinion would not tolerate the existence of professional police, de Veil received payment from secret service funds. He consequently became the first paid, professional police officer in English history, administering justice in much the way a medical general practitioner might deal with patients.

As such, his exploits were many, but throughout his career he remained a one-man show, bearing some resemblance to the famous marshals and sheriffs of the American west. Like most of them he was an individualist who acted alone and never attempted to organize a police force. On occasion he read the Riot Act and, apart from his duties as magistrate, worked as a private detective. Since there existed at the time no police stations, de Veil like other magistrates operated out of his private residence. He finally settled in a house on Bow Street near Covent Garden, where he eventually dealt with cases in four counties and the city of Westminster, but he held no authority in the City of London itself. One of de Veil's various responsibilities consisted of dealing with internal security in wartime, to facilitate which he was given the rank of colonel of militia. Notable success in this aspect of his work led in turn to the reward of a sinecure, that of inspector of imports and exports, a post with a salary but no duties. In 1744, at the age of sixty, he became Sir Thomas de Veil.

De Veil was a type often found most effective in police work, a man who understood the underworld. He showed no fear of organized crime and would make no deals with criminals except to the extent that, as he ended his days a richer man than can be entirely accounted for by the ordinary run of business, he presumably accepted some compensation for selective enforcement of the law with respect to such vices as gambling and prostitution. Indeed, he may have acknowledged as much by the candid comment that his considerable income of no less than £500 per year came from a milieu which produced "the dirtiest money on earth." Yet whatever his limitations, De Veil represents a considerable improvement over his fellow magistrates. He stands as a remarkable individual who fought crime, but as an individual he had no prospect of controlling it in eighteenth century London. Like many outstanding and determined characters he acquired a body of knowledge and skills which could not readily be transferred to a successor. Certainly it seemed unlikely that the contemporary system of patronage appointments would turn up a man of equal ability.

With de Veil the development of police institutions reaches the threshold of modern times. He is in every sense a transitional figure, but the transition from mediaeval to modern practice was protracted, and further evidence of the evolution may be seen in the career of de Veil's even more remarkable successor at Bow Street, Henry Fielding.

CHAPTER II

THE EMERGENCE OF THE LONDON METROPOLITAN POLICE

HE RATIONALIZING, CRITICAL SPIRIT OF the Enlighten-
ment touched nearly all aspects of government in the
eighteenth century. In England it influenced police
arrangements by way of an unusual man, Henry Fielding (1707-
1754), best known to posterity as the author of the novel *Tom
Jones*, who after a short interval following the death of de Veil took
over the Bow Street office. The grandson of a Court of King's Bench
judge on his mother's side of the family, Fielding was born near
Glastonbury, Somersetshire, into moderately affluent circumstances
for many years threatened by the gambling debts of his father, a
veteran of the Duke of Marlborough's military campaigns on the
Continent. Educated at Eton and then at the University of Leyden
in the Netherlands, Fielding achieved some early success as a play-
wright but his satires on Sir Robert Walpole and the Whig ascen-
dancy provoked censorship and at the age of thirty he turned to
the study, next briefly the practice, of law. Unable to make a living
in that profession, he appealed for help to Lord Lyttelton, a friend
from Eton days, who possessed sufficient influence with the Duke
of Bedford, then secretary of state, to secure an appointment as
presiding magistrate in the Bow Street Court in 1748.

Fielding confounded expectations that he would use his
Bow Street position to sell justice in the manner of most contempo-

rary London magistrates. For he was, in fact, an idealist whose satirical plays had been designed to improve public life. He brought his crusading zeal to the office of magistrate, and as a result reduced the income from fees and fines at the Bow Street Court from £500 to £300 a year. Obliged to support a clerk, and his household which included his wife and younger blind half-brother, John Fielding (d.1780), Henry Fielding eventually received some secret service money. But this did not happen immediately and, unlike de Veil, he neither sought nor gained a sinecure.

As a magistrate, Fielding placed his imagination and literary skills at the service of the campaign against malefactors. His first thought was to fight crime through publicity. He encouraged the public to report crimes to Bow Street, including accounts of stolen goods, circumstance of loss and, when possible, the name and description of those believed to be responsible for theft or other offences. It was thus possible to keep a record of crimes and collect descriptions of suspected law-breakers, making a beginning of crime statistics. Fielding published the collected information, together with a running commentary, in the *Covent Garden Journal*, a bi-weekly periodical edited by himself.

The necessity of a real police force became obvious to him, as did the fact that most of the eighty constables in Westminster were of no use. In this matter he found an ally and assistant in Saunders Welch, a self-made individual and high constable of the hundred of Holborn. Service as a constable was for a year, and among those so engaged Welch found six men of unusual promise who agreed to undergo special training and to work without regular pay after their required period of duty terminated. After their year of service they no longer held the power of arrest granted a constable and therefore had only power of citizen's arrest, which left them open to being charged with false arrest if they failed to win a conviction. They were in effect thief-takers who had to work for rewards. Yet unlike ordinary thief-takers they had professional legal instruction and acted under professional advice. Originally they numbered six, subsequently seven, whose existence was unknown to the general public, as was the subsidy Fielding later received from the secretary of state.

London faced a crime wave of unusual proportions when Fielding took office, partly because of unemployed soldiers disbanded

Statuette of a Bow Street Runner.

when the War of the Austrian Succession ended in 1748, and partly because of the prevalence of gin consumption. Fielding met the challenge by publishing, early in 1751, a pamphlet dedicated to the lord chancellor and entitled *An Enquiry into the Causes of the Late Increase of Robbers*. His first point was that while much-cherished freedoms granted by the constitution might protect people against the tyranny of the state, they did nothing to protect them against the more immediate danger of being assaulted, robbed, or worse. He then outlined his views on the causes of crime. Unlike later humanitarians, Fielding did not see poverty as the cause of criminal activity. As England was in fact getting richer, he argued that the desire for luxury, which was harmless in the rich, drove the poor to crime. He opposed not the death penalty, but rather public execution, because it coarsened sensibilities and became a source of entertainment rather than a deterrent. He further believed the rules of evidence to be unfairly weighted in favour of the accused, and contended that mercy was for the most part misplaced in dealing with hardened criminal elements. At the same time Fielding supported public charity, and often dismissed cases of petty larceny when first offenders were involved. However, in the *Enquiry* he did not yet feel bold enough to publicly advocate a professional police force.

Assisted by his clerk, Joshua Brogden, and by Saunders Welch and half-brother John Fielding, Henry Fielding applied himself relentlessly and literally worked himself to death in the course of a few years. He defended his unpopular court decisions in pamphlets, and, like de Veil, did not hesitate to read the Riot Act. Fielding was a dying man when asked to write a report on crime prevention by the Duke of Newcastle, then prime minister. This he wrote in four days, explaining his use of Welch's special constables (afterwards known as the Bow Street Runners), and advocating twenty-four police stations with two constables on duty at all times, with horses provided for their use and authority to travel anywhere in the kingdom. These would in theory be part-time officers, but compensation was to be provided for time spent in unsuccessful pursuit.

In fact Fielding's report was in line with the general trend away from civil servants working for fees, and toward a full-time professional public service. Fielding, nonetheless, remained careful not to go too far beyond public opinion. He understood that elaborate plans, however necessary and sound, would be dismissed as utopian if they put too much strain on ingrained prejudices. He gave an account of his report in his last work, the *Journal of a Voyage to Lisbon*, written just before his death while on the way to Portugal for a rest cure. He died on the 8th of October 1754.

John (later Sir John) Fielding, assisted by Welch and Brogden, succeeded Henry at the Bow Street office. In some respects John's career was even more remarkable than that of his half-brother. He is perhaps the only blind police magistrate in history, and this before the assistance of braille was available. His five year apprenticeship proved adequate and he remained in office until the Gordon Riots in 1780. During this twenty-six year term the Bow Street office functioned with its attached constables, and Welch was made a magistrate. Denied the sense of eyesight, the younger Fielding still possessed a capacity for business. He could dictate correspondence and other documents to a secretary, and possessed a memory for voices which enabled him to identify repeat offenders. Not only did he continue the work of Henry, but added more of a social dimension. John mediated labour disputes, and was able to give more active support to charitable institutions than his brother. Moreover, under him the Bow Street Runners acted openly, regularly receiving a nominal recompense of a shilling and six pence a week, often greatly increased by a guinea a day for detective work with an additional fourteen shillings for expenses. As much crime existed, so did the demand for their services.

Fielding also instituted night-time Horse Patrols. These disappeared upon his departure from Bow Street in 1780, but were revived in 1797 at which point sixty-eight mounted constables, paid two shillings, six pence per night, operated in a five mile radius of the Bow Street Court. They acted in groups of four under a captain, the latter being paid five shillings a shift. Captains carried pistols, the men cutlasses. They patrolled with irregular schedules on varying routes, and worked in close cooperation with innkeepers and those in charge of tollgates, the idea being that the mere knowledge of a real yet unpredictable police patrol in the area would serve as a deterrent to crime.

While the Bow Street system could contend effectively with, if not control, much unlawful activity, it remained helpless against riot. Rioting, as previously stated, was considered a civil liberty by much of the London population, and not itself a crime. Even such a determined, strong-willed individual as Henry Fielding, whose popularity suffered when he passed a death sentence on a rioter, felt it necessary to explain in a pamphlet that the man went to the gallows for being found in possession of stolen goods, and not for riotous behaviour.

Already a social tradition, in the 1760s rioting turned more distinctly political under the influence of the Radical MP, and future London mayor, John Wilkes who, with his organized supporters, on occasion ironically exercised temporary and informal police powers himself. Wilkes demonstrated the impotence of the authorities when he surrendered himself to magistrates after his associates had first, riotously as might be expected, freed him while he was being taken to jail. Contemporary prisons, being run for profit, were in effect criminal hotels where wealthier inmates — of whom Wilkes certainly was one — dined with the warden, while the penniless made out as best they could by waiting on the more affluent. Hence a term or two in jail held little hardship for the Radical leader.

London riots reached a climax in 1780, when Lord George Gordon's anti-Catholic agitation resulted in a bloody and arson-filled three-day upheaval in which the city remained out of control. Since the authorities feared to read the Riot Act, the troops were not called out immediately. Only after King George III threatened to personally read the act if no one else would do their duty, were the magistrates finally moved to action. In this instance Wilkes himself made a novel appearance as a supporter of law and order, and the liberal opposition which previously encouraged him now saw that rioting was a two-edged sword which could serve the cause of bigotry as well as reform. The Gordon Riots counted among their numerous casualties the Bow Street Court, burned to the ground. Sir John Fielding, being away at the time, missed the conflagration, yet with his court destroyed and his health in drastic decline he felt it necessary to resign his office.

The manifest need for effective police in London induced William Pitt the younger, the new prime minister, to introduce a Police Bill in 1785. He did so in the face of continuing strong popular prejudice, and whatever chance the bill enjoyed of getting through as a government measure disappeared when he included the City of London in the project. The City, jealous of its traditional degree of autonomy in police as in other matters, would have none of Pitt's design, and in consequence its opposition sufficed to prevent passage.

Yet Bow Street with its paid magistrates and paid constables had shown the way. A decade later, in 1792, parliament passed the Middlesex Justices Act which in essence multiplied Bow Streets by establishing courts with stipendiary magistrates and paid constables in Middlesex, Kent, Surrey, Essex, and the city of Westminster. These courts had no connection with the City of London and received their funding from the home office, established as a separate department of state in 1782. With the act of 1792 Metropolitan London possessed a police force of sorts, which would be supplemented by the restoration of the Bow Street Horse Patrol, reformed in 1805. The radius was extended to twenty-five miles, served by the recruitment of fifty-seven former cavalrymen, a number soon to grow to a hundred. In 1813 they were taken from the control of Bow Street and placed directly under the home office.

At this time the horse patrol wore blue coats with yellow buttons, red waistcoats, blue trousers, and white gloves. The headdress consisted of a black hat, and the men were equipped with pistols, handcuffs, and truncheons while mounted; and cutlasses when they patrolled on foot. Metropolitan London thus acquired a small group of professionals, but they were in no sense adequate to what was required for the whole city. Yet the Fielding brothers' precedent of a critical, intellectual consideration of police problems was to have successors.

First among these featured Patrick Colquhoun (1745-1820), a successful Scottish businessman with some experience in America, who three times won election as lord prevost of Glasgow. Business brought him to London, where either because of a decline in trade or simply his interest in public welfare, he took a post as a stipendiary magistrate. In this role, and in the manner of the Fieldings, he presented his reflections on police and crime in several pamphlets which gained a wide circulation. The best known of these, his *Treatise on the Police of the Metropolis*, went through seven editions between 1795 and 1806. This work was partly statistical, providing estimates of the size of the criminal population. But Colquhoun withal combined a philanthropic appeal to save the poor from crime, with a practical appeal, pointing out that the cost of prevention was less than the cost of their criminality. He also, in the 1806 edition, presciently proposed the establishment of a police commission board for the whole of London.

At the same time Captain John Harriott, a man of wide travels, by turns soldier and sailor and something of a self-promoter, presented a report to the lord mayor of London with respect to theft on the docks. This finally attracted the notice of the government, and it was in 1798 agreed to set up an office of Marine Police, with Harriott in charge under the general supervision of Magistrate Patrick Colquhoun who two years later produced his own *Treatise on the Commerce and Police of the River Thames*. Meanwhile the new force numbered fifty. It met with immediate success, with losses on the docks falling from £500,000 a year to £100,000, in large measure due to the energy of Harriott who held office for eighteen years. Police work is often most efficient, it would seem, under personalities like de Veil, the Fieldings, or Harriott, known to the public and holding office for long periods of time.

Yet despite the success of the Marine Police, most of British society was still over a generation away from accepting the idea of a professional force. Moreover, during the period of protracted war (principally with France, 1793-1815) and post-war unrest, responsibility for law and order remained for the most part with the military. Their inadequacy in addressing popular discontent was manifest in the inability to control the machine-smashing Luddites, or deal with the attempts at peaceful demonstration which in 1819 culminated in the disaster at St. Peter's Fields, Manchester, subsequently known as "Peterloo." In the latter case, an attempt to arrest a speaker led to Yeomanry cavalry charging the crowd, killing 11, including two women and a child. In coping with terrorism, however, the police were able to uncover and foil the Cato Street Conspiracy, a design to blow up Lord Liverpool's cabinet in 1820, and the most ambitious bid to employ explosives in treason since the Guy Fawkes plot in 1605.

Pitt's adumbration in 1785 having been far ahead of its time, by 1820 the concept of a professional police power had again, and much more generally, reached the political though not yet the popular level. Robert Peel (1788-1850; after 1830, Sir Robert), a Staffordshire squire from a wealthy Lancashire cotton mill-owning family, turned out to be the right man in the right place when he became home secretary in 1822. From the outset Peel worked to simplify, consolidate and mitigate the law in the interests of more efficient and even-handed justice, winning eventual parliamentary approval for extensive prison reform and the abolition of the death penalty for over a hundred offences, while preparing the way for a professional police. As George Howard properly notes in *Guardians of the Queen's Peace*, the fruition of Peel's legal reforms meant that "murder, attempted murder and treason were the only capital offences — a reversion to a state of humane judicial practice which had disappeared from England for nearly a thousand years."

Yet in the event, seven years passed in the home secretary's term of office before he could carry the necessary legislation to create the new police force, first nicknamed "Peelers," and then more enduringly "Bobbies," after their founder. Earlier, during Peel's term as Irish secretary, which began in 1812, he made an effort to establish a rural police force, which will be discussed later.

A London constable, in one of the few extant photographs of the 'Peelers' uniform.

The results were disappointing, but he did not succumb to discouragement. In 1829, with the Duke of Wellington as Tory prime minister, Peel could count on a secure government majority, yet with Pitt's mis-step in mind he took the precaution of excluding the City of London from his scheme. As it stood, a force controlled not by local authorities but by the home office, would be established to serve in Metropolitan London. Everything depended on finding suitable leadership for the new body. In this respect Peel proved highly successful. He particularly detested inefficient patronage, and insisted on putting professional competence before all other considerations when important duties were involved. In a sense, when he chose the right men, his work was done and the ultimate success of the London Metropolitan Police venture ensured.

The selection fell on Sir Charles Rowan (1782-1852), a soldier, and Richard Mayne (1786-1868), a lawyer. In the army Rowan secured his original rank of ensign by purchase, but rose to a lieutenant-colonelcy through merit. He owed much to early training under General Sir John Moore, whose ideas about encouraging initiative in the ranks anticipated those of Lord Baden-Powell a century later. Rowan's knighthood for bravery at Waterloo earlier came through Wellington's recommendation, and the duke now nominated him to Peel. In accepting the suggestion, Peel acquired a civil servant wholly devoted to his work with no family and few recreational distractions. When appointed, Rowan had reached the age of forty-six, having twenty-five years of active military service behind him. Richard Mayne was an Irish barrister, educated at Trinity College, Dublin, and Cambridge, who at the age of thirty-two had become a rising star of the legal profession in northern England. For over a generation he and Rowan were to guide the fortunes of the new force after their appointments as commissioners of the London Metropolitan Police with the powers of magistrates, but holding no courts of their own. This constituted a departure from the Bow Street practice of attaching constables to magistrates' courts. The courts and constables created by the Middlesex Justices Act would remain in being, as would the Marine Police.

The problem was to develop a new force with near-military discipline and dress easily recognized, yet distinct from the army. With this in mind, a uniform design resulted consisting of a blue frock coat with patches bearing the division number and individual constable's number on the collar, with brass buttons, blue trousers and top hat bearing the letter "P" for police. The men carried no firearms or other deadly weapons, merely a baton for self-defence while a rattle, for summoning help when needed, hung from a broad leather belt. A dark brown overcoat served for winter wear, and whitish trousers were worn in the summer. This outfit cost £6 which the police officer paid through deductions from his salary of three shillings a day. On leaving the force a constable might hope to recover part of the cost of his uniform by reselling it to the tailor contracted to supply the police regulation clothing.

Three shillings *per diem* in fact represented the pay of an army sergeant who would, in theory, make the ideal policeman, having the toughness of the rank and file and, at the same time, an air of authority and some experience of responsibility. "Gentlemen" rated as being in most cases too refined for the rough and tumble of police work. Yet in the event, former soldiers, considered the best material available, did not make up the majority of early recruits. There would in fact be a considerable turn-over of personnel in the early years, drunkenness being the major cause of resignations and dismissals. The force was first divided into six divisions, each in charge of a superintendent. Assisting the six superintendents were twenty-four inspectors and ninety-six sergeants, the total force being nine hundred and ninety.

Rowan and Mayne met their initial challenge in resisting considerable pressure from influential people to make the expected political appointments. Recruits had to be literate, under thirty-five years of age, at least five feet, seven inches in height, and able to offer two references from those deemed gentlemen. But in any case, they joined an institution which could not hope to be immediately popular. It faced the obvious hostility of the criminal classes, and indeed of numerous ratepayers who saw the force as a useless expense. Surprisingly, many of the wealthy also expressed hostility in that they feared the police would restrict their liberty and interfere with their privileges. There existed the enmity of the force created under the Middlesex Justices Act, who now saw the new body as ultimately displacing them. Peel's force would operate at first in a radius of seven miles from Charing Cross, its personnel having the title and powers of arrest possessed by the old parish constable. There existed no pension for years of service or for those injured in the course of duty. Promotion was to be from the ranks, with no provision for officer training, but ranking military officers might be seconded to the police.

London Metropolitan Police headquarters became popularly and even semi-officially known as Scotland Yard, so named because the site, whose street address is 4 Whitehall Place, originally was the residence of the Scottish ambassador (and Scottish kings when they were present in the English capital). New Scotland Yard, the present police building, dates from the 1890s, and is supplemented by another structure, Scotland Yard North, built in 1939. Assistance from Scotland Yard may be requested by any force in Britain, if so desired. Such assistance commonly involves specialized detective work, but London headquarters were not at first identified with such endeavours. Crime detection in fact met an early set-back due to the efforts of an over-zealous constable who attended a Chartist meeting in plain clothes. This led to charges of spying on the public, which had obvious disadvantages. But it nevertheless became a practice to take selected officers off routine uniformed patrol work and other duties, and assign them to the collection of criminal intelligence. By 1842 a number of men were given permanent assignments as detectives, who among other things bought information from informants. The home office offered rewards for information leading to the conviction of wanted criminals until 1892. After this, rewards could still be offered by private agencies, but a police practice which flourished in the age of the eighteenth century thief-takers had come to an end.

The first need of the London Metropolitan Police — to acquire the respect and confidence of the public — proved to be difficult work. Instructions given to constables from the outset included an exhortation to be civil and obliging to persons of all ranks, and not assert authority without reason. Above all, they should not provoke or insult the public. To many of the latter, however, the police simply represented a new version of the impotent watchmen and as such commanded no respect. Constables who did "assert" themselves in the line of duty were sometimes charged with brutality, while the City of London, being beyond their jurisdiction, found itself a refuge for criminals on the run.

Another handicap arose when Lord Grey's unsympathetic Whig government gained office late in 1830 and Lord Melbourne replaced Sir Robert Peel as home secretary. Yet the Whigs, under pressure to abolish Peel's creation, understandably resisted doing so in a period of heightened mass unrest and agitation for parliamentary reform which sometimes threatened revolution, as the unpopularity that went with maintaining law and order could now be adroitly shifted from themselves to the police. For four years (1829-1833) the new force lived through what might be called its "heroic" period before signs appeared of a favourable change in the public attitude. But in the interim a large turn-over in personnel resulted as constables gave up the struggle for respect.

Outside London there still existed no professional police. The calling out of the army to control threatening or violent demonstrations still often ended with bloody results. Property could not be adequately protected, and there were casualties when troops fired into crowds. In the capital a different situation prevailed.

A watchman in London, seen outside his box, which functioned as both a resting place for him and as a cell for prisoners. He is equipped with a lantern, a stave, a sword and a rattle.

Among the Radicals, Francis Place, master tailor and co-founder of the Chartist movement, early realized that the political success of mass demonstrations depended on the control of extremists and reckless trouble-makers lest their excesses obscure the justice of the cause and alienate those who were otherwise supportive. Place saw the police as allies rather than enemies, and advised the free use of batons — particularly the baton charge — as the most effective, relatively humane, means to control unruly demonstrations. But he recommended that arrests be avoided when possible, as they too often led to complicated and pointless legal proceedings. Place's advice undoubtedly made an impression, and when police repeatedly clashed with mobs there were bruises and some broken bones and bloodied heads on both sides, yet no fatalities among those on the receiving end of the law officers' batons. London in the 1830s — a decade of agitation which did not stop with the passage of the Parliamentary Reform Bill of 1832 — remained a reasonably orderly city with no recourse to the military, while troops dealt with more deadly riots in the provinces.

Ultimately the public's sense of fair play came to the rescue of the police, the occasion being a riot at Cold Bath Fields, London, in May 1833. Home Secretary Melbourne ordered the force to disperse a demonstration but, contrary to practice, neglected putting his order in writing. Consequently the men appeared to be improperly acting on their own initiative, without due authorization and therefore with personal responsibility for whatever occurred. In the ensuing confrontation, which ended in a pitched battled of an hour's duration, one constable was stabbed to death and two seriously wounded. The press initially attributed the violence entirely to police provocation and brutality, the coroner's jury at an inquest bringing in a verdict of justifiable homicide in the case of the policeman who had been killed. This led to an appeal, and an independent investigation whose report indicated the ambiguous, compromised role of the home secretary. So many of the public took this as a sufficient vindication of the police that common opinion finally started to turn in their direction. By degrees they were seen not only as victims of prejudice and political-bureaucratic evasion with respect to the Cold Bath Fields incident, but more generally viewed as a body of men who had obviously reduced the incidence of crime and controlled rioting without inflicting serious casualties. The London Metropolitan Police were there to stay and would gain in popularity with the years.

The problem of population growth outstripping municipal boundaries and services, including police, could be found in most provincial cities. But it was by no means restricted to them. The City of London itself, once one of the better-policed parts of the greater metropolitan area, soon became a sanctuary for crime as police pressure drove criminals there from surrounding districts. A clear case emerged accordingly for the adoption of the more efficient London model throughout England, and a tentative step in this direction came a year after Cold Bath Fields when, acting on the recommendation of a report, the Bow Street Patrol and the constables organized under the Middlesex Justices Act amalgamated with the London Metropolitan Police.

But it was also evident that because of logistical considerations and regard for provincial traditions of independent identity, local police authorities would have to be under local county and municipal control and not, like the London Metropolitan Police, be placed directly under the home office. The Municipal Corporations Act of 1835, which abolished old municipal oligarchies and set up elective councils, facilitated matters and placed the professional police question on the national agenda, yet there resulted no immediate rush to adopt the London system.

The first scheme for establishing a nation-wide police force arose out of a commission, headed by the Benthamite Radical Edwin Chadwick, which recommended that such law enforcement personnel be recruited and trained by the home office. Chadwick's plan, presented in 1839, never enjoyed much chance of acceptance because, apart from other considerations, Chadwick himself was seen as the main author of the New Poor Law of 1834, one of the most unpopular pieces of legislation in British history. The New Poor Law, which replaced traditional outdoor relief with "union" poorhouses where the able-bodied indigent of several parishes were compelled to reside and work (the other choices being begging, crime or starvation), thus indirectly but fatally prejudiced Chadwick's police measure. Yet even had he been a more popular man, there still existed powerful local interests which would have defeated any project for externally imposed police.

As an alternative, and in its way a compromise, parliament in the same year (1839) passed the Permissive Act which encouraged local authorities to establish and maintain paid, professional constables. Under its terms the home office supplied trained constables only if and when requested, while acquiring the right to occasionally inspect, but not recruit or daily direct, local detachments. The quality of local police hence depended on the practice of those who employed them. In some instances London-trained personnel duly engaged to organize and train provincial contingents; in others neighbourhood residents were hired without much regard to qualifications. While in some of the more remote hamlets a one-man force might still be a paid and uniformed version of the old casual parish constable, the Permissive Act nonetheless met widespread, if less than universal, positive response and in large cities

London standards of efficiency were developed and maintained. Indeed, even the City of London accepted the necessity of organizing professionally, though it did not abandon its customary particularity by integrating with the London Metropolitan Police. Instead, while remodelling, the City retained its own force which remains independent to this day.

Elsewhere, the pressure to appoint professionals remained unabated, as crime migrated to the areas which retained the old voluntary system. Not until 1856 for England and Wales, and 1857 for Scotland, however, did parliament pass the County and Borough Police Act which made the adoption of paid police compulsory, though leaving them under local authority. By degrees a force of almost twenty thousand came into being, all required to meet the standards of the home office. The great achievement between 1839 and 1856-1857 was the extension to the countryside of an unarmed, civilian but uniformed type of policeman throughout all of Britain. This, in essence, was the force that moved into the twentieth century, acquiring along the way new branches for such problems as political subversion, and traffic control.

In a free society there are no laws against political opposition or even agitation. By the same token, demonstrations in nineteenth century Britain were legal if peaceful. But problems arose in the case

A group of London constables in the mid-nineteenth century.

of terrorism or riot, and at the time parliament passed the Permissive Act, England faced the threat of the physical force wing of the Chartists. The Chartist movement, designed to secure universal manhood suffrage by a monster petition, was organized in 1838. Shortly thereafter, its moderate founders, Francis Place and William Lovett, lost control to the Irishmen Bronterre O'Brien and Fergus O'Connor. These men, who learned the art of politics in Daniel O'Connell's Catholic Association, introduced machine-style operations which bore some resemblance to those of Tammany Hall in the United States. They never intended to actually lead an uprising, but were given to violent speeches and threats of force. After the parliamentary rejection of the petition, however, a real physical force wing emerged. It had no central leadership, or network of organizers, but did drill in secret, collect what arms it could gather, and fashion pikes. With regard to the latter, physical force pamphlets often stressed the effectiveness of the pike and weakness of regular troops in street fighting.

In London a police capacity for effective response existed, though an early attempt to employ it elsewhere led to a singular failure. As railways made quick transportation possible, in the troubled year of 1839 the home office sent a detachment of sixty London Metropolitan Police constables to Birmingham. Taken from their local environment this force proved completely ineffective, and had to be rescued by the army when they lost control of a Chartist crowd in the Birmingham Bull Ring. But the unfortunate Birmingham episode aside, elsewhere outside of London authorities still as noted depended virtually exclusively on the military when riots threatened. In the north, the formidable General Sir Charles Napier, later a pioneer in organizing police in India, had the Chartists under control. He managed this by inviting their leaders to a demonstration of cannon fire, pointing out how efficiently marching columns could be shattered by artillery, then routed by a cavalry charge. Accordingly, no trouble ensued in the north, but in Wales, which lacked an effective military command, a small Chartist rising came to a head. A local leader, John Frost, organized several hundred Chartists who moved into the city of Newport armed with pikes, only to be quickly dispersed by a volley from twenty-eight soldiers, supported by some special constables, billeted in the railway hotel.

Chartism went into an eclipse after this for nearly a decade, but then re-emerged, reaching a peak in 1848, a year of revolution on the Continent and in Ireland. A monster demonstration was planned, with the intention that over one hundred thousand would gather to present to parliament a petition bearing more than five million signatures. Such numbers went far beyond what the five and a half thousand London Metropolitan Police could control. The presentation was accordingly forbidden, though at the same time an appeal to the public produced a hundred and seventy thousand special constables. The position of special constable dated from the reign of Charles II. Special constables, used not long before against Frost's attempted insurrection at Newport, were given the full powers of a regular constable for a limited time, and worked under the authority of a magistrate. Although all were volunteers in 1848, this temporary service could be made compulsory.

As matters developed, Fergus O'Connor was called in and warned by the police, but it was finally decided to let the demonstration go ahead. On 10 April 1848, the chosen day, only twenty-five thousand gathered, and it turned out upon examination that there were less than two million signatures on the petition, numbers of them in the same handwriting and some, the names of famous historic individuals or characters in fiction, even more obvious, if perhaps weakly humorous, forgeries. The Duke of Wellington called out the troops but kept them out of sight, and no need arose for their services. The special constables, carrying the main burden of crowd control, out-numbered the demonstrators, and no violence occurred.

The question of terrorism proved more serious, as the moral support of the public did not suffice to prevent terrorist activity. This problem came to the fore in 1865 when the Fenian Brotherhood, a trans-Atlantic Irish secret society, was responsible for the deaths of twelve people during an unsuccessful attempt to rescue Richard Burke, one of their leaders, from Clerkenwell Prison in London. A clear need existed for the sort of specialized intelligence-gathering agency with respect to state security and politically-motivated violence which could not be supplied readily by the conventional detective force established in 1842. The ultimate response was the Special Branch Section, formed under control of the home office, which faced the challenge of the so-called Dynamite War launched in 1883, again by Fenians.

No Criminal Investigation Department (frequently referred to as the C.I.D.) to handle the more difficult or sophisticated cases of "ordinary" non-political crime existed until 1878, when it was placed under a director also in charge of all detective forces in the London Metropolitan Police. Detective stories beginning with Sherlock Holmes have made the words Scotland Yard synonymous with the C.I.D. which today as before handles matters which county and borough police find beyond their resources; hence references to "a case for the Yard."

The long-standing problem of riot control became urgent once more after the passage of the Damages Act of 1886, which made the police liable for damages done to property by rioters. The occasion for the measure was rioting along Pall Mall, where many of the more exclusive London clubs have their establishments, after the rowdier elements of the crowd had been effectively excluded from a peaceful demonstration in nearby Trafalgar Square.

With the new century came changes and new challenges. The Women's Volunteer Police appeared in 1917 (renamed Women's Police Service the following year), adding a feminine presence as a temporary wartime measure which evolved into an integral part of the police force throughout Britain during the 1920s. Near the end of World War I there also came a three-day police strike for union recognition which was not granted, though a grievance board resulted and conditions of service improved. A strike of London and Liverpool police in 1919 proved more serious, but soon collapsed. Dismissals of strikers followed in consequence, but again grievances were remedied. Police remained on duty during the General Strike of 1926 when special constables again made an appearance, as indeed did the army.

Britain's acceptance of professional police was late, centuries behind France, but Continental police have remained apart from the community, and rarely achieved popularity or become the heroes of fiction. The British police experience was a logical development of common law, and professionalism could not, given public opinion, have been introduced much earlier than 1829. The secret funding by government of the activities of de Veil and the Fielding brothers was helpful but inadequate, as was the multiplying of the Bow Street model under the Middlesex Justices Act of 1792. Professional police were first introduced in London, where the greatest need existed, and ten years elapsed before the provinces made an effective beginning. By mid-century or very shortly thereafter, most of Britain benefited from new, improved police protection and the debate with defenders of the old, essentially mediaeval system of voluntary constables ended legislatively in 1856 with the County and Borough Police Act, which extended and standardized professionalism. The next year Scotland also came in line with the same regulations, by means of which local authority recruited and controlled the force, but inspection by the home office ensured the maintenance of standards.

Like all human institutions, the London Metropolitan Police have, and have had, their faults; but they were and are the best example of a professional police force which serves the public. Consequently they have served as the model for all societies in which common law tradition prevails. They proved that it could be done.

Van for taking offenders to jail, Glasgow, early twentieth century.

CHAPTER III

THE RISE OF THE NEW YORK POLICE DEPARTMENT

HE AMERICAN COLONIES CONSTITUTED THE most numerously populated area living under common law outside of the British Isles. While the Revolutionary War of 1775-1783 severed political ties with the crown and empire, it left intact the colonial institutions of local government and if anything strengthened the traditional English hostility to most forms of regulation, including police. Indeed, the prejudice against professional police was from the outset even stronger overseas than in Britain. For one thing, the American Continent was far more insular, being separated from Continental Europe by an ocean instead of a channel. For another, a substantial portion of the colonists came to the new world to escape from what they deemed the excessive restrictions of the old one, and were deeply imbued with a prejudice against state interference of any kind.

Survival early demanded militia service against Indians, and with it supposedly a modicum of subordination to military authority, but both during and for generations after the colonial period most North American militias bore a notorious reputation for indiscipline. Nonetheless, the Indian wars brought about the legal obligation to serve in the militia when it had lapsed in England itself. Unease, however, remained. For example, as early as 1637 efforts to foster greater military co-operation amongst militia companies met rejection by Governor John Winthrop and the common council of Massachusetts on the grounds that they considered "from the example of the Praetorian band among the Romans, and Templars in Europe, how dangerous it might be to erect a standing authority of military men, which might easily in time overthrow the Civil Power." The Revolution further encouraged this attitude, and in 1784 the Continental Congress stated that standing armies in peacetime "are inconsistent with the principles of Republican Governments, [and] dangerous to the liberties of the people."

Yet common law tradition reinforced by a classical education proved to be an inadequate preparation for the realities of colonial and early post-independence American society. Fear of the military by degrees gave way to necessity, as substantial steps were taken to establish a federal standing army by 1790; but the invincible prejudice against professional police would survive at least another half century until the first steps toward a London-style system were taken in 1845.

At first there scarcely seemed to be a police problem, because traditional English institutions in most cases sufficed for small, largely rural, communities. Moreover where the need arose, as in how to address the matter of an unwanted stranger entering a community, or a local resident taking up known or suspected criminal activity, colonial ingenuity invented the mythical "Squire Birch." In this procedure the party deemed undesirable received notice to leave, signed by Squire Birch. If they failed to comply within a reasonable time they would be unceremoniously run out of neighbourhood. This informal and illegal means of crime prevention — and rough justice — perhaps served well enough in intimate, socially homogeneous communities, but it had the disadvantage of being a primitive form of vigilanteism which was habit-forming and would have more serious consequences when frontier society developed diversities and complexities. Further, the Squire Birch treatment became less and less relevant as town size and social heterogeneity increased. In seaports and in large cities it could not be applied at all; these had to get along with the mediaeval system of policing brought to America by the English colonists.

The seaport of New York, originally New Amsterdam and capital of the Dutch colony of New Netherlands, later long the acknowledged metropolis of America, may be taken as a typical colonial city.

Dutch municipal institutions roughly paralleled the English, the *schout* being the equivalent of the constable who served under a magistrate, and New Amsterdam from early days maintained a watch in a cosmopolitan milieu. Eighteen languages were spoken there by the 1640s; and, while initially an effort was made to keep visiting boisterous seamen on board ship rather than spending the night in town, this understandably proved to be a losing battle. Further, the existence of a slave population in the city posed an internal threat while, until the end of the century at least, hostile Indians constituted an external one. The Indian danger in particular induced Peter Stuyvesant, New Amsterdam's last Dutch governor, to form a burgher guard, followed in 1652 by the organization of a rattle watch composed of a captain and eight men as a defence against night attack.

Considering the potential difficulties, the transfer of jurisdiction from the Dutch to the British administration in 1664 transpired comparatively smoothly, and the rattle watch survived until 1682. In the first several decades after the arrival of the British regime, however, New York not only grew in size but became increasingly a government town. Economy dictated that soldiers, who in any case had to receive wages, should take over the duties of a paid citizen's watch, and the ability to lean on military support would delay the adoption of better police arrangements in eighteenth century New York, and indeed later in nineteenth century Montreal. By 1680 New York was divided into six wards with a constable in each. When the civilian watch was restored briefly in 1684, eight men were assigned to a ward, and paid twelve pence each: a much higher wage than that of the London Charlies, but New York prices also ran higher. Until the disbanding of this force in 1689, New York ranked as one of the best-policed towns in the world.

The same year — 1689 — marked the beginning of a long series of trans-Atlantic conflicts ending with the annexation of Canada to the British Empire in 1763. Throughout this period the military served as New York's police in wartime, with the civilian watch restored during interludes of peace. The key document for the city's municipal government (including police arrangements) in the eighteenth century and to some extent even later, was the Montgomerie Charter of 1731 which provided for a permanent civilian watch, all male citizens being obliged to serve or hire a substitute. A list of those eligible to serve was kept by the aldermen of a city which then numbered about ten thousand. The Montgomerie Charter remained on the books after the Revolution, to be invoked by a mayor of New York City in 1857 during a dispute with the governor of New York State. It is important to understand that the city charter was granted by the legislature of the British colonial province, later the American state, of New York at Albany; and thus could be amended by the governor and state assembly.

Eighteenth century New York already had a substantial black population, for the most part slaves or former slaves. White society consequently lived in permanent apprehension of a racial insurrection and, above all, a slave revolt. A slave uprising in 1712 was followed by a more serious one in 1741, the latter being suppressed with special cruelty as several of the perpetrators were burned at the stake. The slave revolt of 1741 produced panic and a temporary militia guard, though palpably the majority of New York's citizens were neither willing to pay for an adequate police force nor provide one through their own service in an unpaid watch. This difficulty was partly resolved when the governor of the province, at the request of the city's common council, in 1747 provided a company of fusiliers from the British garrison to patrol the city; this body remained in service until the end of the war period in 1763. Yet the citizen watch established by the Montgomerie Charter survived in theory by the grace of paid substitutes, who proved no more satisfactory than the London Charlies. With the close of hostilities with France, a paid watch of sixteen was organized, provided with "centinal" (i.e., sentinel) boxes. Pay was £32 a year, but it remained a watch, with nothing but a citizen's power of arrest.

The British wartime regime between 1776 and 1783 saw police work again revert to the military, once more with unsatisfactory results. A virtual population exchange occurred, with Patriots leaving the city while Loyalist refugees moved in. The Loyalists attempted to organize a civilian watch with, by 1778, some eighty men patrolling the streets under the direction of a committee of three appointed by the army commander. After the departure of the crown forces and before the new civic administration established itself, a brief period of disorder ensued during which the Continental army acted in a police role. Things then settled down. New York from 1790 to 1820 remained relatively free of crime and tumult in spite of the fact that the population rose from thirty-three thousand to a hundred and twenty-three thousand. The old system of constables and watchmen, supplemented by a force of paid marshals, seemed adequate. The war in Europe (1792-1815) virtually suspended trans-Atlantic immigration, the existing population being augmented by natural increase and heavy immigration from elsewhere in North America.

During these years there emerged at least one police personality, Jacob Hay, who bore some resemblance to de Veil. He held the office of high constable of the city of New York, and had the difficult task of enforcing laws passed by a state legislature at Albany which reflected more closely the Puritan attitude of the rural population than it did the practices of urban New York.

Although life and property were reasonably secure, breakdowns of law and order did occur. In 1806 a Protestant Orange Lodge attempted to parade through Greenwich Village, then an Irish Catholic suburb. The ensuing clash took the life of one watchman and injured several others, the military finally restoring order. Fatalities also resulted in the course of attacks on would-be doctors when, in 1788, it was discovered that certain medical students were, with the connivance of some physicians and teaching hospitals, robbing fresh graves to secure bodies for dissection. The students, after being arrested for their own safety, found themselves in the city jail besieged by an enraged lynch mob, with the first effort of the military to rescue them beaten back. In the end, after the soldiers shot and killed several of the attacking mob, the students availed themselves of discreet police-assisted exile as an escape. Such disturbances, however, were only a taste of those to come.

Serious trouble began in the 1820s when massive Irish immigration, now largely Catholic, brought pressure on a still mainly Protestant community. To begin with, hostilities arose with the blacks whom the Irish drove out of domestic service and, to a large extent, from work on the docks. Similar to eighteenth century London, theft on the waterfront became commonplace. Moreover, centres of crime and vice developed, like the Five Points, on the lower east side. By the 1830s, riots, usually featuring Irish immigrants struggling for a place in American society, reached epidemic proportions.

As the city limits were fixed by the state, the jurisdiction of the mayor and common council was extended and urban life moved northward. This meant that the number of watchmen could be increased with the size of the city. Since they served from sundown to sunrise, they could and did follow other occupations. Their pay of seventy-five cents a day equaled that of a London constable in 1829 (three shillings); but, still exercising no power of arrest, they remained without professional pretensions. By the mid-1830s they numbered about four hundred. Appointments were both political and subject to the consent of the common council, which often meant that they were made at the ward level by the elected aldermen and assistant aldermen. Marshals in theory constituted a more efficient instrument than watchmen since they had the power of arrest, but in practice they were not normally available for patrol, being fully occupied delivering summonses or attending at court. Their appointments came from the mayor though a state law limited the number of marshals to a hundred at any given time.

Patrick Colquhoun's writings did not pass unnoticed in the United States. They found an adherent or at least an imitator in Charles Christian who in 1812 produced *A Brief Treatise on the Police of New York*, but no compelling need for change existed at the time. Yet once the London police were in being, New York had an example which could be followed, for criminality and social disorder in New York by about 1830 approached the abysmal situation of eighteenth century London. Apart from frequent riots which required the use of the military, the city suffered from a cholera epidemic in 1832 and a major fire four years later. The looting which accompanied the fire did much to underline the need for police. As things stood there existed no means of crime prevention, since constables and marshals would not act until a crime was committed. The constables were unpaid while the marshals, working for fees and rewards, like the English trading magistrates and thief-takers before them understandably competed with one another, and did not share information acquired in the course of their work. As goods were often recovered by the marshals without convictions, it seems likely that collaboration existed between the police and the underworld.

The danger to the general public was brought home in 1842 by the publicity attending the case of Mary Rogers, whose body was found floating in the Hudson River some days after she left her mother's boarding house on her way to work. Rogers was well known to a number of prominent New Yorkers as "the pretty cigar girl" because she sold cigars in a fashionable tobacco shop. Among those acquainted with her was the Baltimore native, poet and fiction writer Edgar Allan Poe, who dramatized the disappearance and murder in *The Mystery of Marie Roget*. Poe, who thought himself something of an amateur detective, transferred the scene of the crime to the more romantic atmosphere of Paris. Using imaginary names he worked out his own improbable solution, but the real case was never solved. Indeed no agency existed capable of carrying out a proper, professional investigation.

Politicians were by this time prepared to take up the question of establishing a professional police force, and the public was prepared to listen. Yet this involved more than the mere overcoming of a prejudice against police, and three years of preparation, with numerous proposals and counter-proposals, followed before the force came into being. From the start, Protestant Whigs and nativist "old Americans" feared domination of the police by the Democrats and the political patronage machine of Tammany Hall, who both represented the despised Irish Catholic immigrants. Yet in the end the Democrats prevailed, a force being established with George Matsell, a Democrat, as chief of police in 1845. Appointment was by the mayor and common council, which in practice meant by the ward aldermen. Tenure would likewise be at the pleasure of the mayor and council, which again translated into determination by local politics.

George W. Walling, himself later chief of police, described the manner of his recruitment: "One day, late in 1847, I was hunting in New Jersey, when a friend approached me, and asked whether I would like to take his place on the New York police force." Duly nominated by an alderman and assistant alderman, Walling was sworn in by the mayor. As he further explained, "The men at that time owed their appointment entirely to political preference; there was no surgeon's inspection, nor any civil service examination. In fact no attention was paid to the physique or mental acquirement of the applicant."

No uniforms were worn by the men, who carried batons, often concealed, as were the star-type identification badges issued

to them. The pay was good: $1500 *per annum* for the superinten-
dent; $700 for captains; $600 for assistant captains; $550 for
sergeants; and $500 for patrolmen. In all, eight hundred were
recruited for a city of over six hundred and thirty thousand; and
ten years later, when the population stood at about seven hundred
and eighty thousand, the force had increased to twelve hundred.

At this time approximately half the city rated as foreign-born,
mostly Irish, and when the second generation is considered, it is evident that New York had become a predominantly Irish town. The old
Protestant American element was in retreat but still controlled the
state government at Albany most of the time. The underworld
included thousands of child criminals, and of the estimated ten thousand prostitutes most were teenagers or younger. Gangs such as the
Bowery Bouhys thrived, and supposedly responsibly civic-minded
institutions like volunteer fire departments fought one another for
recreation. As in London at the turn of the century, river thieves
flourished in the harbour area, being if anything even more given to
promiscuous violence, including murder, than their English counterparts. George Walling wrote that, "It made no difference apparently
to these criminals how little money or how few valuables their
intended victim had about him." Chief Matsell argued for the necessity of water police, but none were organized until 1858.

In view of such disorderly conditions the creation of the new
police body, for all its limitations, represented a substantial if somewhat
belated achievement. Whatever its flaws, most blatantly those created
and exacerbated by political patronage, New York as of 1845 probably
possessed the best force in the United States. As was typical in United
States jurisdictions, police of officer rank were elected, a practice of
dubious merit and efficiency indeed shared by the personnel of the
judiciary. Reform in New York was slow but forthcoming; tenure was
soon extended to two years and by 1853 to good behaviour.

George Matsell provided an element of continuity and
steadiness to the fledgling force. He stands, considering the conditions in which he worked, as a good policeman, yet more in the
manner of de Veil than of the Fielding brothers since he retired with
more wealth than he could possibly have acquired on the salary of
a chief of police. For that matter, although well paid by contemporary standards, the police worked long hours, still resembling the

mediaeval village constable at least inasmuch as they were given responsibility for sanitary arrangements and other matters which interfered with their routine duties.

As the effectiveness of patrol depends largely on a known and visible presence, the absence of uniforms set limits to what the force could accomplish. Hostility to the wearing of uniforms derived partly from a fear of being identified as a policeman on inconvenient occasions, and partly from the Anglo-American reluctance to be associated with things military. The argument for uniforms gained ground when, in 1853, the journalist J.W. Gerard pointed out, amongst other things, the success and public acceptance of uniformed private police at the New York Crystal Palace Exhibition. Soon after a blue frock coat was authorized for general police wear. Resistance followed, involving several dismissals from the force for refusing to wear the required garb. The police administration took the matter to court and won a decision whereafter uniforms finally became the order of the day. Efforts to get the city to pay for the contentious clothing came to nothing, as it was argued that police salaries, for a constable then being $700 per year, were sufficient. There still existed no provision for pensions or compensation for those injured in the line of duty, nor for their families if they were killed. However, in particular cases individuals or their families might be voted small sums for injuries suffered during service.

While uniforms undoubtedly enhanced the prestige of the police in some quarters, the force in its early years paralleled the London Metropolitan Police in that it enjoyed no widespread popularity. The principal charge against them, levied by the Whigs and Native American party, was that of Irish exclusivity. Matsell, in response, offered figures to prove that the foreign-born on the force were the same percentage as the foreign-born in the general population. This may have been true, as many of the Irish were by then second generation.

With the growth of such Irish influence, there was sooner or later bound to be a full-scale conflict between Albany and New York City. Nor is it surprising that this confrontation should arise in the 1850s during the term of office of Fernando Wood, a Democrat, the first professional politician to become mayor of New York. Wood centralized the police under his own command by control of appointments to a police board, and he encouraged the positive image if he did not originate the slogan of "New York's finest." During his tenure of office the police for the first time wore their uniforms with pride, as by now the military for the most part also did. For a while, Wood's crusade against vice won the support of the more respectable section of the population — especially Whigs and Native Americans — who normally would have voted against him.

Wood undoubtedly believed himself to be a reformer, but he remained a politician for whom patronage was the price of survival. His difficulties were three-fold: how to enforce laws, passed by a temperance-minded state legislature at Albany, which were substantially unenforceable in New York City; his campaign against vice had to be selective as he was not strong enough to consistently interfere with the illicit pleasures of the rich; and finally, at election time he needed alike the financial support of the police force, their votes, and their tolerance of plural voting, part of the game of machine politics. "Voluntary" contributions to campaign funds were enforced by such means as keeping non-contributors on duty for twenty-four hours at a time, while tolerance of plural voting remained notorious. Wood's selective suppression of vice was soon exposed in the press, while to evade temperance laws he insisted that it was unlawful to forbid the sale of imported spirits because they were taxed. These transparent evasions and devices provoked widespread ridicule and gave Albany the incentive to take over control of the police.

The long-expected crash came in 1857 when the Republican governor, John A. King, decided to use his authority to take control of the New York Police. A simple take-over proved to be unconstitutional because of the existing Montgomerie Charter, so King created a police zone of several counties comprising New York, Brooklyn, Westchester, and Richmond (Staten Island). This arrangement bore some resemblance to the London Metropolitan Police, with the state of New York playing the role of the British home office. The difference was that the Republicans, who controlled the state government, still used the force for patronage. Under King's scheme nine commissioners, seven appointed by the governor and one each by the mayors of New York and Brooklyn, controlled the police. Three of the governor's appointees were to be from New York State, putting the city's members in a minority.

King's failure to appoint Democrats to the commission further underlined the politically partisan nature of the body.

Wood protested the unconstitutionality of the entire proceeding and on these grounds, not waiting for a court decision, simply ignored the authority of the commissioners. He argued that like the City of London, New York City should have its own police. Invoking the Montgomerie Charter of 1731, he claimed the legal right to appoint a watch; then declared the New York Police to constitute such a watch, and consequently to be under his control. Individual policemen in the city faced the unenviable choice of whether to obey the mayor on one side, or the commissioners (and by implication the governor and state assembly), on the other. Understandably, they divided almost entirely along political lines, the Democrats who made up the majority of the force supporting Wood. In all, about eight hundred stood by the mayor, and some three hundred with the commissioners.

Both groups claimed the legitimate control of all police stations and telegraph apparatus, the telegraph having been introduced in the early 1850s, a decade before London. Even more complete confusion resulted when the mayor named three hundred men to replace the state supporters, while the commissioners presented 800 to replace Wood's adherents. Among the state supporters was George Walling, then a ward captain, given a warrant to arrest Fernando Wood. The mayor defied Walling's authority, after which, as the discomfited police officer later explained: "I went round the desk to take hold of him; he ordered me away and struck the office bell. It brought Captain Anderson, of the Municipals, who had adhered to Wood's usurpation. He and his men grabbed hold of me at Woods' order, and forcibly ejected me from the office." Soon fifty state reinforcements advanced toward City Hall to carry out the arrest, but they, too, ran into superior numbers loyal to Wood and were driven off.

At this point the 7th Regiment of the New York National Guard happened to be marching down Broadway, en route to an exhibition in Boston. The commissioner called on them for help in the name of the governor, ultimately their commanding officer; the Guard obeyed orders and duly proceeded to City Hall. Wood, seeing the futility of further resistance in the face of *force majeure*, submitted to arrest. The victory of the state forces was soon confirmed by a Supreme Court decision, and the Metropolitan Police took over. A period of confusion and re-adjustment followed and the force remained understrength for over a year. This the underworld exploited to the full, and riots still demanded the intervention of the military.

As the habit of criminals using such lethal weapons as pistols and knives was now common, there was in response talk of issuing sidearms to the police. Officialdom long publicly rejected the policy, but informally it for the most part quietly tolerated reality when officers with their lives on the line began buying and carrying concealed handguns for their own protection. In fact with the New York force particularly in mind, the Colt Firearms Company soon produced their Pocket Police Model revolver, a compact, lighter five-shot .36 calibre variation of the larger, six-shot .44 calibre Colt Model 1860 Army, a military service weapon. In spite of this, however, there was neither training in the use of firearms nor authorized general arming for the New York Police until 1895.

The departure of Matsell, who sided with Wood, from office left the force without a police personality. Three years elapsed before another effective chief appeared in the person of John A. Kennedy, a Republican but somewhat incongruously a friend of Thurlow "Boss" Tweed, leader of the Tammany Hall machine who was in turn surprisingly an enemy of Fernando Wood. Kennedy found an able assistant in Thomas Acton, a member of the police board and also a Republican. Despite a continued barrage of politically-motivated Democratic criticism, the Metropolitan Police proved to be an improvement over the institution which existed during Wood's administration. The resulting adoption of state-controlled forces in twelve major cities as far afield as Boston, New Orleans and San Francisco is telling testimony to the success of the model. Further, New York Harbour Police were at last introduced, while the relatively new invention of photography was employed to set up a rogue's gallery. George Walling (now Captain Walling) reorganized the detective branch, which numbered twenty-four with a minimum of four men on duty at all times. Detectives were the one section of the whole force who officially carried firearms, and by now the only one still in plain clothes.

It was this relatively strong organization which faced new responsibilities imposed by the outbreak of the Civil War in April 1861. As de Veil learned in London over a century earlier, in wartime all duties not assigned to, or at least not assumed by, other agencies fall to the police. In a New York context this included secret service work, amongst other things providing presidential security when Abraham Lincoln passed through Baltimore en route to Washington in 1861. When Kennedy's assistance was requested, he sent Walling and a force of departmental detectives to Baltimore where, along with the Pinkerton Agency, they uncovered and foiled a plot to kill the president. Despite legal difficulties, arms and other supplies destined for Confederate ports were held in New York. Counter-espionage presented special difficulties as Southern residents or sympathizers in Union territory could not be treated as enemy aliens without recognizing the Confederacy's independence, though in the end a few of those under suspicion were compelled to go abroad.

Since ordinary means of recruiting did not fill Northern military requirements once the early enthusiasm for volunteering wore off, Kennedy and his police became *de facto* recruiting agents. Because rewards were given for men enlisted, this endeavour proved profitable, if additional work. Kennedy in 1862 became a district provost marshal, while the New York force were likewise given the paramilitary status of a provost marshal's guard, making them responsible for the arrest of all military deserters including, what became particularly important, the capture of bounty-jumpers — those who enlisted for a bounty and then deserted, often re-enlisting under another name for another bounty.

The great test of the Metropolitan Police during the Civil War came in the summer of 1863, when conscription came into operation. Politically, most of the Catholic Irish as War Democrats opposed the secession of the Southern states but were equally opposed to the abolition of slavery. Their voluntary military enlistment in the Federal forces in proportion to their numbers exceeded that of any other identifiable ethnic group in the city, but they reacted violently against the draft. Although the wartime economy made for full employment, rising prices at the same time depressed the standard of living. Irish racial antagonism to blacks, and hostility to them as competitors in the labour market, was explicit and of long-standing, being declared openly in the Irish community's newspapers. Moreover, because of the slavery issue blacks and abolitionists were widely blamed (and not only by the Irish) as being causes of the bloody conflict threatening to split the nation.

The National Conscription Act became law on the 3rd of March 1863. Under it, substitutes could be hired for $300, an amount far above what the vast majority of the Irish (and for that matter most other immigrants and citizens of whatever background all over Union territory) could afford. A deep resentment ensued in New York City as elsewhere, which the governor of New York State and many leading Democrats across the North did nothing to diminish by publicly announcing their opposition to the draft throughout the spring and early summer. Moreover, if serious rioting or other illegal anti-conscription manifestations occurred, not much assistance could be expected from the military as the most effective of the Union forces were fully engaged several hundred miles to the south. Then, at the end of June, the Confederate Army of Northern Virginia slipped around the west flank of the Federal Army of the Potomac and thrust north up through Maryland into Pennsylvania. There followed the momentous three day contest at Gettysburg (1-3 July), when the future of the Union was rumoured to be in the balance. And ten days later the United States' largest city underwent a severe, equally long trial of its own.

The regular troops in the Eastern District which included New York City were under the overall command of General John Ward, a veteran of the War of 1812. A lawyer in peacetime, General Sanford led the state militia, while the immediate officer in charge of the regular troops in the city was Brigadier Harvey Brown. Ward placed Brown under command of Sanford, whose first thought was to protect the armouries. Happily, Brown ignored Ward's order and concentrated his troops at police headquarters on Mulberry Street. On the 12th of July (the anniversary of the Battle of the Boyne in 1690, always a time of heightened Irish sensibilities), the drawing day for the draft, every reason existed to expect some trouble, but no forebodings prevailed as to any overt challenge to the civil authorities. Consequently Kennedy did not take the precaution of ordering a general alert and, in the event, the 12th of July passed without serious incident. However, real trouble began the next morning. As news of disorder reached police headquarters via the telegraph, Kennedy ordered small detachments to protect draft enrollment stations, and all reserve platoons in Brooklyn and New York were called in.

Meanwhile, predominantly Irish crowds collected and armed themselves with cudgels and other weapons in many parts of the city, finally concentrating in Central Park. Attacks on draft registration offices began on Third Avenue, where the ten or so police on duty were unable to prevent the burning of the building. When Kennedy,

alone and dressed in civilian clothes, arrived on the scene, he was recognized and severely beaten by the mob. Amid physical blows and
verbal abuse, he managed to reach a nearby Central Park pond and,
on swimming across, was rescued by a friend. Lucky to be alive and
in no condition to continue the direction of affairs, he relinquished
command to Thomas Acton, who proved equal to the task.

Acton concentrated his forces at police headquarters, sending out flying columns to endangered points. As there were thirty-
two precincts linked by telegraph to the central command post, he
for a time remained instantly informed of trouble and capable of
quick response — until the mob destroyed most of the telegraph
lines. Acton did his best, but when the rioting became general could
not cover all threatening situations. Most serious was the burning of
a coloured orphan asylum at Fifth Avenue and Forty-Third Street.
When the inmates were brought to George Walling's station on
Thirty-Third Street between Eighth and Ninth Avenues, "the poor
creatures," as he put it, "were almost crazed with terror, and ... glad
enough when, after the riots were over, arrangements were made to
convey them to a temporary home on Blackwell's Island."

Later on the first day of disorder, the 13th of July, Walling intrepidly led a hundred of his men against a crowd of two thousand ram-
paging at Forty-Fifth Street and Third Avenue. His orders had a virtually

Burning of the Provost-Marshal's office, New York, on the first
day of the Draft Riots.

A lynch mob during the draft riots.

military ring to them: "Kill every man with a club. Double quick, charge." In Walling's words, "We took no prisoners, but left the rioters as they fell. The number of broken heads was large. The mob dispersed in all directions." New York's Draft Riots of 1863 lasted three days, in which the police with some help from Brigadier Brown's regulars won most of their battles, but could not prevent the burning of station houses on East Twenty-Second Street or East Eighty-Sixth. Nor did they prevent the lynching (including the torture and mutilation) of many blacks as victims of anti-draft hostility, or the widespread incidence of looting. With the Battle of Gettysburg over the military arrived from Pennsylvania, but the troubles had run their course and the danger was over.

The Draft Riots were undoubtedly the finest hour of the force, which had taken the brunt of the shock with only marginal help from the army and indifferent support from the civil authorities. Politicians, as in the case of London's Gordon Riots, once again proved reluctant to jeopardize their popularity by associating their names with strong measures against even the most violent public disorders. The Metropolitan Police lasted another seven years after which, in 1870, the City of New York resumed control of its force. While the Metropolitans undoubtedly represented a higher degree of professionalism than Fernando Wood's men, they were still part of a patronage system. But apart from politics, the New York police faced a permanent condition of social instability produced by the continuous flood of unassimilable immigrants into the city.

The restoration of municipal control over the force did not result in immediate and extensive change in personnel as the police had tenure. Nor was there any change in the character of the city one year after the mayor resumed his authority and eight years after the Draft Riots of 1863 when, in 1871, New York suffered its last major upheaval of the sort. As mentioned, as early as 1806 a clash occurred between the Orange and the Green on the 12th of July, anniversary of the Protestant victory on the banks of Ireland's River Boyne. The planned Orange parade of 1871 was first banned by Mayor A. Oakley Hall, acting on the advice of Superintendent James J. Kelso. The banning of the parade raised the question of civil liberties, and when the matter became controversial Governor John Hoffman overruled the city authorities, leaving them to take what precautions they could against anticipated trouble. These were extensive. Veteran Inspector George Walling was put in charge of police, while three regiments of the National Guard were called out, the 6th, the 9th, and the 84th, under command of a general officer. Together the military and police outnumbered the Orangemen as they marched north on Eighth Avenue, amidst the abusive shouting of on-lookers.

Serious trouble began around Twenty Fifth Street when police charged the rioters who assailed the Orangemen and their protectors with stones and bottles. There were still no signs of a major disaster until someone fired a shot from a window. At this the men of the 84th Regiment delivered a volley into the crowd without waiting for orders. Being equally harassed, the 6th and 9th Regiments also opened fire. Of the crowd and by-standers, one hundred and twenty-eight were either killed or wounded, leaving the march to continue without further interference. The risks of using even regular, presumably reasonably well-disciplined troops for crowd control should have been obvious; the increased danger inherent in using militia, which the National Guard essentially were and are, approached the borderlines of criminal folly. Yet there was a circumstance present — the widespread distribution of firearms amongst the population — which was not a factor in London or most other European cities or even, to the same extent at least, in Montreal.

Technologically, New York, a pioneer in introducing the telegraph in the 1850s, proved one of the last to utilize the telephone which did not become general for the police until after the turn of the century. Pay continued to be high, reaching a maximum of $1400 in 1894. Pensions would be paid to the families of those killed in the line of duty or who were disabled or died with over ten years' service. All policemen could retire on half-pay after twenty years, retirement being mandatory at the age of sixty.

Superintendent George Walling retired in 1885 and published his memoirs two years later. He observed therein that a well-connected officer of the British Brigade of Guards convicted of assaulting a constable found himself duly sentenced and imprisoned, in spite of the intervention of influential friends. In a similar case when a well-known New York City gambler and politician assaulted an officer, no charges followed, and the constable in question found himself transferred to another possibly less attractive station. Walling's final comment on American policing was pointed: "While I admit that, as a nation, we have the best form of government there is in the world, under our municipal system in New York there is less liberty and protection of property, than in any city in Europe, Russian cities not excepted." He blamed political interference in the force, which undoubtedly was the heart of the matter. But for all that New York provided a generally effective police who like their London counterparts managed to survive and flourish amid a society which had behind it a strongly entrenched hostility to police or government interference of any kind.

New York's professional police emerged in 1845, only sixteen years behind their London counterparts. Had it been possible to free them from political control, they might well have reached London standards. Certainly chiefs like Matsell and Kennedy were men of outstanding ability. Yet even with external control the force would have to face problems unknown to the London police, like successive waves of immigrants, or enforcing liquor laws unacceptable to local inhabitants. Although New York had greater problems the police-civilian ratio was lower there than in London, and the police-civilian ratio did not keep up with the expanding population. Policing was easier in London than in New York, yet if it had been politically possible, an externally-recruited and externally-controlled force on the London model would in all likelihood have made New York a more law-abiding city in the last century.

CHAPTER IV

POLICE IN MONTREAL

ONTREAL AND NEW YORK ARE both seaports, gateways to the interior of North America and subject to the related pressures of continuous immigration. But they are nevertheless very different cities. For one thing, Montreal is today predominantly French-speaking, though in the mid-nineteenth century census counts revealed a slight English-speaking majority. Yet the key to understanding the differences in the development of their police institutions is not to be found in their ethnic-linguistic disparities, but rather in the comparatively over-size presence of the military garrison in Montreal.

In 1760, at the end of the French colonial regime, Montreal was a city of five thousand with a swollen wartime garrison of a thousand men. The French army could easily carry out police work in the city, as was indeed done by British troops during the war years in eighteenth century New York. In rural areas the police responsibility rested with the captain of militia who had no real counterpart in the English colonies. Under the French system the captains of militia were less than a justice of the peace and far more than a constable, being appointed by the intendant who controlled not only police but the administration of justice and finance for the whole colony. New France, often facilely described as "feudal," was in spite of seigneurial land tenure a centralized bureaucracy in most essentials of government. The English colonies to the south, more egalitarian in outlook, were paradoxically also more feudal inasmuch as local government was in the hands of local landowners, part-time amateurs, under the supervision of a governor and elected assembly. Yet the bureaucratic character of New France notwithstanding, no substantial effort was made to transfer the elaborate police system in contemporary France to the New World. Indeed, in a colony with a population of sixty-five thousand or so little reason existed to do so.

With the coming of the British regime, many seigneurs became justices of the peace, thus acquiring power in local government which they never exercised before. The city of Montreal itself possessed no municipal charter, being governed by the quarter sessions of the county of Montreal. These assemblies of justices of the peace and grand juries managed such matters as lighting, sanitation, and police responsibilities until Montreal formally became a chartered municipality in 1832. In that year the city numbered about twenty-eight thousand, and the garrison some five hundred. A watch-style civilian police was created which at the time of its demise in 1837 numbered twenty-eight, though from the beginning members of Montreal's British garrison performed informal police duties when they chanced across crime in progress. Perhaps the most notable instance of this *ad hoc* police function occurred about 1800 when Henry Hardinge (then a youthful ensign in the Queen's Rangers but later a distinguished officer on Wellington's staff in the Peninsular War, a politician of ministerial rank, a viscount, and governor-general of India), one evening drew his sword to disperse a gang of thieves assaulting the Scottish merchant Edward ("Bear") Ellice.

Early nineteenth century Montreal received two streams of immigrants, one from the predominately French-speaking countryside, the other mostly from Britain and Ireland. In the course of the 1830s the overseas stream predominated and began to shift the cultural balance of the city. By the 1840s there were about seventeen thousand French- and twenty-three thousand English-speaking inhabitants of which some nine thousand were Irish. Although complex, the causes of the Rebellion of 1837 owed much to the ethnic shift in Montreal's population. One consequence of this was the emergence of a large, vocal Irish Catholic minority, whose spokesman was Daniel Tracey, allied to the nationalist Patriote party led by Louis-Joseph Papineau. An 1832 west ward by-election in which Tracey, previously jailed in Quebec City for libelling members of the provincial legislative council, challenged the U.S.-born businessman Stanley Bagg who stood for the British or Constitutional party. This contest provided the occasion for the first serious Montreal political riot which, in turn, engendered a new bitterness which grew as the decade advanced. Hitherto relative electoral peace had prevailed in the west ward because of a tacit understanding that one seat would go to the English interest, the other to Papineau who personally represented the riding since 1814. But Tracey's bid broke the agreement, and the special police constables (initially a hundred, eventually two hundred and seventy-five in number) sworn in by the magistrates, normally relied upon to control unruliness at elections, proved less and less effective as the month of May went on. Elections, which were by open ballot and occupied periods of up to several weeks, often involved intimidation of voters and frequently violence, there having been a major riot in Quebec City when the first election was held in 1792. Yet plainly the west ward by-election was now one of particular difficulty.

Resort to the military for help at election time in Montreal was still considered a reluctant last choice, but on the evening of the twentieth of May the magistrates finally appealed for the assistance of the main garrison at the Quebec Gate Barracks. Lieutenant-Colonel Alexander F. Macintosh, the commanding officer, exhibited the professional soldier's dislike for police work, especially in circumstances where serious injury or even loss of life seemed in prospect. Yet whatever his misgivings he could not refuse to aid the civil power. He sent to the fort on St. Helen's Island for two six-pounders and their Royal Artillery gun crews, also ordering out troops from the 15th (East Yorkshire) Regiment and activating the local volunteer Royal Montreal Cavalry. Late afternoon the next day the reading of the Riot Act made little noticeable impression on a mixed Irish and French Canadian crowd, and when the East Yorkshires with unloaded weapons moved in on Place d'Armes and St. James Street, they were met with showers of stones in an on-going two-way conflict as members of the Constitutional party bombarded their opponents in front of the soldiers with missiles. Only the Patriote side attacked the troops, however; and Macintosh, after repeated warnings to the hostile crowd, ordered the troops to load and subsequently shoot not by volley but man by man, the better to maintain fire control and minimize casualties. The mob dispersed, but not before three French Canadians lay dead on St. James Street.

Macintosh, Captain Henry Temple of the 15th Regiment and two magistrates — Dr. William Robertson and Pierre Lukin — subsequently found themselves arrested for murder, with Papineau both publicly and privately unsuccessfully trying to persuade Macintosh to name the magistrate by whose order he opened fire. All charges were eventually dismissed as the Riot Act had been duly read and other procedures properly followed, but bitter political partisanship henceforth held sway making any fair police function difficult for the civil authorities and destroying the impartial credibility of the military with the Patriotes and their sympathizers. Matters drifted toward insurrection or potentially even full-scale civil war. During the next five years increasing politically-motivated breakdowns of law and order occurred in Montreal as the British party, their physical force wing first organized as the Dolphins and then more generally as the Doric Club, regularly brawled and sometimes rioted with their counterparts in the Club de Patriotes.

In April 1837 the twenty-nine man city police force was dismissed when the current funds for its maintenance ran out. With but a few months to go before the outbreak of rebellion, Montreal, with a population approaching forty thousand, so far as the regular civil power was concerned could rely only on its local magistrates, the sheriff and the high constable. A real, functioning police force no longer existed even in theory, though in emergency recourse could be had to the temporary expedient of swearing in special constables or calling out the volunteer militia. By autumn the provincial constitution was suspended and Montreal's Municipal Charter of 1832 withdrawn. Attorney-General Charles Richard Ogden took up residence in Montreal in November, assigning local police responsibilities to the Royal Montreal Cavalry, the volunteer unit called out five years previous. With them there served two future chiefs of police, Captain Charles Ermatinger, and Thomas McGrath.

The Rebellion of 1837, centred in the Richelieu River Valley and in the Lake of Two Mountains region in its Lower Canadian aspect, was essentially a matter of military operations carried on outside Montreal. But the speedy suppression of active insurrection in the countryside still left the problem of post-rebellion policing of the disturbed areas which remained locales of discontent and conspiracy. The military wished at all costs to avoid this task, as there was an obvious danger of the emergence of the sort of conditions which later plagued the American South during the Reconstruction years.

Soon after his arrival as governor in 1838, Lord Durham consented to a police ordinance proposed by Ogden, the attorney-general, and Sir John Colborne, commander of the army, creating a new Montreal force of a hundred and two men with four mounted patrols, and Pierre Leclerc, a French Canadian Loyalist, as superintendent. This body, increased to a hundred and twenty, remained under Leclere for two years when stringent financial retrenchment led to the reduction of its personnel to sixty, and its budget from £10,046 to £3,504. In February 1842 Lieutenant-Colonel William Ermatinger, who had served in the Royal Montreal Cavalry like his brother Charles, took over as police commissioner, soon combining the offices of inspector and superintendent. He held this position for the next fourteen years, during which time his was the most dominant figure in Montreal police affairs. The son of a North West Company (Nor'Wester) fur trader father of Swiss descent and an Objibwa mother, he was perhaps from an early age somewhat familiar with Montreal's governmental bureaucracy since his uncle, Frederick William Ermatinger, held the offices of the city's postmaster and sheriff, 1810-1827; but the study of law equipped him more properly for his subsequent career. So, too, especially considering the potential of Montreal society for internecine strife, did his service with the British Legion in the Carlist War in Spain, where he had an opportunity of seeing the horror of total civil war first hand.

The city of Montreal force was supplemented by a rural police establishment built around fourteen stipendiary magistrates or paid justices of the peace, who each commanded a small detachment of full-time, uniformed personnel quartered in barracks. This body owed something to the inspiration of the Irish (subsequently

Royal Irish) Constabulary organized in 1836 (See Chapter V); and to Colonel George Cathcart who had served in Ireland and more recently in Jamaica where a military police force had been constituted. Lieutenant-Colonel Augustus Gugy, a French-speaking Protestant of Swiss descent, held command of this rural Lower Canadian paramilitary force which covered only the disturbed areas in the vicinity of Montreal and was in no sense a provincial police. Of the fourteen stipendiary magistrates, most were either regular military officers seconded to police work, or militia officers associated with the suppression of the Rebellion of 1837. But they were not organized in time to set up an extensive or effective intelligence service, so that the outbreak of a second rebellion, in November 1838, caught authorities by surprise. This attempt, which included an invasion from the United States, fizzled out in the face of the overwhelming strength which the crown could put in the field.

In their role as conciliators the stipendiary magistrates enjoyed a large measure of success, leaving behind no legends of exploitation by carpet-baggers such as a generation later would characterize the Reconstruction era after the American Civil War. In St. Hyacinthe, for instance, the local magistrate, Lieutenant Thomas Rainsford, was assured by a former insurgent officer that he had the good will of the local population. The paramilitary force these magistrates officered, however, was understood to be temporary, and was for the most part disbanded in 1840. Gugy found himself in charge of the reduced Montreal police, while Leclere, who had hitherto commanded, was given a post as magistrate at St. Hyacinthe.

Gugy not long after achieved promotion to adjutant-general of militia, his successor in Montreal after a brief interval being Lieutenant-Colonel William Ermatinger who took office as commissioner of police and remained in control for the next twelve years. As commissioner of police, William Ermatinger's jurisdiction covered the entire island of Montreal and the adjacent parishes of Laprairie, Longueuil, Boucherville, and Ile Perrot. Under him served three chief constables, one French, one Irish, and one English. There were five mounted constables which with fifty-two foot constables made up a force of fifty-seven. Like the London police they were paid three shillings a day, in this case to guard a city of about fourteen thousand inhabitants. Under Ermatinger were Captain Charles Wetherall, who had served as a stipendiary magistrate; and Thomas Wily, former colour sergeant of the 83rd Regiment, who had been commissioned in temporary provincial regiments raised during the troubles of the late 1830s. This force, although professional and apparently impartial in its conduct of affairs, was nevertheless staffed entirely by those who had helped put down the Rebellions of 1837 and 1838.

A military garrison of up to fifteen hundred remained and the year 1841 saw a new unit raised to guard government property and, if necessary, the frontier with the United States: the Royal Canadian Rifles. Recruited from British regulars who after their assigned term of imperial duty preferred to remain in Canada, like the provincial regiments raised during the Rebellion the Royal Canadian Rifles were intended for North American rather than general service. There was not to be another rebellion, but the fifty-seven man Montreal police force would require military support to handle election riots and the largely Irish canal workers in the Beauharnois and other areas.

In 1843 William Ermatinger, backed up by a detachment of the 71st Highland Light Infantry, read the Riot Act to Irish Canadian labourers on the Lachine Canal. This occasion led to the creation of a special ten man police force to patrol the canal and its immediate vicinity. At Lachine the canallers were simply quarreling among themselves, possibly as a consequence of the perennial clash of the Orange and the Green; but three months later the Beauharnois Canal workers raised demands for better working conditions. This proved more serious as a detachment of thirty soldiers was surrounded and overpowered on the 12th of June 1843. A second nearby confrontation the same day resulted in the reading of the Riot Act, followed by the troops opening fire. One canaller died on the spot, with five more mortally wounded.

An inquiry acquitted the military of misconduct in this matter, but they were less fortunate during the election riots of the following year, 1844. The occasion was a by-election contest between William Molson and Thomas Drummond with Irish nationalists acting as conspicuous partisans of Drummond and French Canadians divided. In spite of the presence of the military and elaborate precautions, one French Canadian was killed when he incautiously grabbed the bayonets of two soldiers, and died of his wounds after being stabbed by a third. Molson withdrew under protest and Drummond carried the day one thousand three hundred and three votes to four hundred and sixty-three. During the general election of 1844 police were barred from the polling areas, lest they appear to influence the results. This placed the responsibility for keeping order entirely on the military. Disorder nonetheless occurred though no casualties resulted, and the troops found themselves accused of siding with the government candidates. In the municipal election of 1844, soldiers were again called out in what had become a matter of course. One man was killed and there were nineteen arrests. No riots transpired in 1845, and only minor disturbances in 1846 and 1847. On the whole Montrealers seemed as much given to riot as New Yorkers, and like New Yorkers could not be controlled without military intervention. The Montreal police proved useful but not sufficient in 1845, the same year that the first professionals appeared in New York.

The year 1848 is one of the most important in Canadian constitutional history, as it saw the introduction of responsible government and the coming to power of the Reform administration of Robert Baldwin and Louis-Hippolyte La Fontaine. The Loyalists who put down the Rebellions of 1837-1838 no longer commanded the provincial government, yet they still controlled the police force and the militia. Moreover they were stronger in Montreal than in most of the rest of the province as a slight English-speaking majority existed in the city. Such was the background for the crunch which came in 1849 when the Baldwin-La Fontaine government introduced the Rebellion Losses Bill, permitting former Rebels to receive compensation for property damages. A statesmanlike measure of reconciliation, it nonetheless could not but be regarded as anathema by many of the English population of Montreal who bitterly considered it a reward for treason and a betrayal of sacrifices made for the crown and the British connection.

After a brief residence at Kingston, the seat of government of the United Provinces of Upper and Lower Canada moved to Montreal where the assembly, with its Reform majority, consequently became subject to the pressure of the local population who already possessed a history of riot. Abundant reason existed to expect more of the same, but the officers of the garrison remained wary of taking responsibility for police work and would under no conditions take the initiative. Signs of trouble appeared when Police Magistrate Charles Wetherall found it necessary to order troops out to dismantle an as yet unmanned barricade in Place d'Armes. However, La Fontaine, who as attorney general had the power, hesitated to make wider use of the military although the existing seventy man police force had never been effective in riot control.

Tension mounted as the city waited to see if Governor General Lord Elgin would sign the bill after its passage through the assembly, and thus make it law. This he did on the 25th of April 1849, arriving at the legislature in what amounted to a surprise visit, informing neither assembly, police nor military of his intention to approve the measure. He hoped thereby to psychologically disarm the hostile part of the population with an accomplished fact. But the element of surprise did not last long, and Elgin departed amid a shower of eggs and other as yet relatively benign missiles accompanied by the violent verbal abuse of those who now felt betrayed by British policy in general and the governor in particular. He made it safely back to his western suburban residence at Monklands (later transformed into the Villa Maria girls' school), where the guard detail was hastily reinforced with a company of the 23rd Regiment in readiness to withstand attack should it come. Meanwhile an incensed crowd gathered around Parliament House, located in St. Ann's Market, while Thomas Wily, acting on Ermatinger's orders, rallied constables at the danger point.

La Fontaine finally agreed to call out the troops, but this required a number of tedious bureaucratic procedures. It was first necessary to secure the approval of the mayor, then the commander of the forces, and finally the town major. By the time Ermatinger and Sir Charles Gore, commander of the forces, reached the residence of the town major, the crowd had broken into Parliament House and set it on fire. Troops arrived in time merely to hold on-lookers back from the fire and enable the firemen to prevent the spread of the blaze which consumed the building. Ironically, the destruction of property, especially the library, exceeded what it was proposed to pay to Rebellion Losses Bill claimants.

For the next few days members of the government relied on troops for their personal protection. Such protection could be provided, but again property did not fare so well and, besides doing more minor damage elsewhere, a mob burned the stables as well as destroying the furniture and library of a new house belonging to La Fontaine. The obvious course for the government, as it could not indefinitely rely on the military, was the formation of a special police force. La Fontaine accordingly appointed a former deputy adjutant-general of militia, Lieutenant-Colonel Etienne-Pascal Tache, to organize and arm a body of five hundred special constables. This amounted in effect to arming one party against another, and soon angry demonstrators marched on Bonsecours Market where Tache was drilling his men. Soldiers prevented a clash, but the crowd of some three thousand dispersed only upon assurance that the special constables would be disbanded. This was done, though hostile mobs still roamed the streets.

When Elgin returned to town on the 30th of April to receive a vote of confidence from the assembly, despite heavy military protection he faced on his departure a much more serious attack than the one experienced five days earlier. Instead of eggs and the like, stones were now thrown over the heads of the soldiers at the governor and his carriage by the mob. Elgin accordingly sought to return to Monklands by an indirect, elusive escape route, while members of the crowd got into cabs and attempted to cut off his retreat. The object of their outrage personally again got through to his residence unscathed, but Ermatinger and several of the cavalry escort, as well as their horses, were injured by rocks.

In light of such events and the failure of the special constable attempt, the need for the creation of a provincial police became more manifest than ever. La Fontaine acceded to the raising of a fifty man mounted paramilitary corps on the model of the Irish Constabulary, supplemented by a hundred foot police, all on the provincial budget. Placed under the command of Captain Charles Wetherall, with instruction to be provided by recently discharged non-commissioned officers, this new force had its first station at La Prairie south of Montreal, across the St. Lawrence. Training began in May 1849 and the Constitutional or British party lost no time in deriding those enlisted as "Elgin Guards," amongst other things.

Montreal Chief of Police Thomas Wily resigned in protest against
the creation of a politically partisan body, but the city remained
quiet until mid-August when nine men suspects in the burning of
Parliament House were arrested.

La Fontaine, anticipating another attack on his house in the
St. Antoine suburbs, requested police protection. But he also took
the precaution of gathering together at the residence a small force
of armed supporters, including Doctor Wolfred Nelson, the commander of the Patriotes at St. Charles in 1837. Troops arrived on
the scene only after a volley from the La Fontaine house had put to
flight a mob numbering some two hundred two to three hundred.
At least five of the latter were wounded, and one, an eighteen year
old youth, fatally. Efforts to bring the mounted constabulary across
from La Prairie the next day (the 16th of August) proved abortive
in the face of hostile demonstrations. After this the city corporation
swore in two hundred new special constables of a more obviously
non-partisan character, and their moral force, assisted by riot
fatigue, produced a return to relative tranquility.

At this point the Constitutional party, better known as the
British party, played into the hands of La Fontaine by becoming
associated with the Annexation Manifesto. This document, signed
by most leading members of the embittered Montreal business
community, in words "more in sorrow than in anger" called for
annexation to the United States. Signers were in consequence
deprived of militia commissions and government office, the patronage being acquired by Reformers. The Provincial Mounted Police
finally moved from their base at La Prairie to assume duty in
Montreal in November 1849, but were disbanded within a year on
the ground of expense. At the same time the Provincial Cavalry,
which had served as back-up for the municipal police, was taken
off the imperial budget and likewise disbanded — ostensibly also
because of economy, though its Loyalist associations were
undoubtedly a significant factor.

Although clearly unable to control the city's endemic riots,
and suffering demoralization from the resignation of Thomas Wily,
the municipal police were left to do the best they could. On the
positive side, William Ermatinger, who possessed considerable
ability and remained over-all police superintendent amidst many

difficulties until 1855, organized a Water Police contingent of thirty men. The latter, mostly former soldiers or Irish Constabulary, brought a new element of law and order to the docks and canal shipping, yet the police as a whole remained in a poor position to deal with the challenge posed by the general election of 1851 and government reluctance to call upon the military. The new mayor, Charles Wilson, took the initiative, swearing in three hundred special constables enlisted from among those considered "respectable householders" to act in concert with another two hundred also hired to assist the regular police as needed. In turn, a new confidence asserted itself as officers intrepidly arrested known bullies and trouble-makers immediately upon any manifestation of lawlessness. With this change to an active police policy, and the moral support of the press, the election of 1851 passed without serious incident.

After a period with no permanent (still less any effective) chief of police, Captain Charles Ermatinger succeeded Thomas Wily in the office, thus serving under his younger brother, Superintendent William Ermatinger. For several years things settled down, with the force clearly in competent hands. But trouble was again expected; and trouble came in 1853 when apostate Roman Catholic priest Alessandro Gavazzi on the 9th of June arrived to give an anti-papal lecture in Montreal. There had been a riot a few days previous when Gavazzi appeared at the Presbyterian Free Chapel in Quebec City, and he came upriver protected, it was said, by an armed guard of Orangemen.

The intention was for Gavazzi to speak at Zion Congregational Church near Hay Market, only a half mile from the main military base at the Quebec Gate Barracks. Charles Ermatinger took the precaution of posting fifty men of the regular city police outside the church, reinforced for the occasion by eighteen Water Police. Further, in company with Mayor Charles Wilson he requested and received a contingent of one hundred troops to be kept out of sight in a nearby fire engine house, in case of need. But unfortunately the Gavazzi lecture coincided with a change in military personnel, the 20th Regiment of Foot being replaced by the incoming 26th Cameronians, and most senior officers, lulled into a false sense of security by the relative civic peace which had prevailed for nearly four years, were at the docks bidding farewell to the former garrison.

While Gavazzi delivered his usual passionate denunciation of Roman Catholicism inside the church, a mostly Irish Catholic crowd of several hundred tried to break into the building. They, and the protecting police, soon became embattled. This continued for over an hour as the police cordon held amidst a shower of stones, at which point gunshots began to issue from both the crowd and the church door. The exhausted constables, armed only with batons, now fell back to reform their increasingly battered ranks, but the mayor had seen enough and called on the Cameronians in the engine house to make their appearance. The troops, under the command of a colonel, a captain, and two lieutenants, loaded and primed their weapons before rather than after advancing into position — a somewhat unusual step in the circumstances, as the act of loading in plain view of a mob was a warning which often had a cooling effect on its members. The soldiers moved into the square before the church, then turned ranks outward, about fifty paces between them back-to-back. Half confronted the demonstrators who had regrouped after falling back in the direction of the fire engine house, and half faced towards the Zion Church building.

Order returned until the end of the lecture, when the audience began to leave the building. As they moved toward the troops for protection, the military personnel in the opposite line came under attack by stones, shots also apparently being fired in their direction. Mayor Wilson quickly read the Riot Act, after which a party unknown (but most probably a civilian former non-commissioned officer with a parade-square voice) gave the order to fire. The Cameronians obeyed despite the prominent efforts of at least two of the nearest officers, Lieutenant Robert Quarterley and Captain Charles Cameron, who both attempted to stop them. Cameron, particularly, did so at some danger to himself, moving along the firing line striking the men's muskets up with his sword. Four civilians were killed on the spot, five mortally wounded, and about a dozen others more or less seriously injured. The police had clearly lost control of the situation, yet most public indignation again fell on the military though a protracted series of inquiries produced ambiguous results. For some days unarmed Cameronians walked the streets at their own peril, while the city's Protestant minority, about seventeen thousand out of approximately fifty thousand, felt insecure.

During the remaining eighteen years of the British garrison's presence in Montreal there occurred no serious breakdowns of law and order. The department was by this time moving away from its military origins, and taking on a more North American character. By 1861 a constable's pay reached a dollar a day, still starkly inferior to the $2.00 to $2.50 wage of the average labourer. Under these conditions there existed not only increased temptation to accept bribes, but it proved difficult to keep personnel of quality on the force, and it was not uncommon in the 1870s to have fifty men out of the approximately one hundred and fifty total complement resign in a single year. Ste. Cunegonde district constable and famous strong man Louis Cyr, who subsequently went into the hotel, gymnasium and circus businesses, could augment his meager police salary with public exhibitions of his remarkable physical power, but his good fortune was somewhat singular. Chief of Police F.W.L. Penton, born in France of an English father and a French mother, argued strongly for higher wages and the creation of a police reserve. Meanwhile periodic complaints about the ineffectiveness and openness to bribery of the Montreal police were not followed by much official responsiveness to the obvious need to increase their pay. But for all that they did their duty at least as efficiently as most of their North American counterparts.

Although the Quebec City and Halifax police also in their origins owe something to a significant military presence in their communities, the average Canadian city does not. Toronto, which then had a population of five thousand, acquired a full-time high constable upon incorporation in 1834. The following year five full-time paid constables were hired, with a reserve of fourteen specials. In 1859 the high constable was renamed chief constable, as the force grew with the city. On the whole Canadians perhaps showed somewhat more respect than New Yorkers did for police authority, and for law and order — or at least their riots tended to be less bloody — but as the history of nineteenth century Montreal indicates, they were in no sense an especially law-abiding people.

CHAPTER V

RURAL POLICING IN IRELAND: THE ROYAL IRISH CONSTABULARY

RELAND IN THE EIGHTEENTH AND nineteenth centuries featured English common law and police arrangements in the English style, while possessing a different social system. In the cities the London model of unarmed police sufficed, but the social-religious violence of rural Ireland demanded an armed paramilitary police. Effective means of organizing such a body were not found until 1836. Once established, it was to become the paradigm for colonial police forces in India, South Africa, Australia and Canada, and to some extent for the state troopers which emerged in the United States in the twentieth century.

A major part of the problem in the Irish countryside originated in the fact that most landlords (substantial numbers of them absentees and some of them British) were Protestant but, except in heavily Protestant Ulster, most peasants were Roman Catholics. Exacerbating this there further existed difficulties involving all classes of rural society, regardless of religion, because of over-crowding on arable land and the absence of tenure for Irish tenant farmers. Faced with chronic social volatility on such a scale, it is not surprising that the combination of justice of the peace and parish constable which on the whole maintained reasonable law and order in the English countryside had no chance of equal performance in Ireland. In 1773 some effort was made to remedy this through the creation of police at the baronial level. Each barony, a rough equivalent of the English hundred and like it under a high constable, was initially assigned four sub-constables. Later attempts to reform the Baronial Constabulary by increasing their numbers and officially scrutinizing their qualifications could not change the fact that they were under-paid (£20 *per annum*) Protestant political patronage appointees who at their best rose to the watchman level.

Given these circumstances, peasants organized secret societies that could under favourable conditions informally take over much police power. Such bodies were partly agricultural trade unions in function, but also significantly more. They exhibited the character of clandestine guerrilla or terrorist units which, usually nocturnally, attacked landlords' property and livestock (and sometimes the landlords themselves or, more commonly, their agents and unpopular tenant farmers), as well as terrorizing other peasants competing in the over-crowded agricultural labor market. Denominational strife between Protestants and Catholics often figured prominently in these nighttime raids, yet open, more or less pre-arranged daytime brawls between bands of agricultural laborers at fairs and other social events also constituted a recognized recreation. However, when on occasion secret society predators got seriously out of hand, troops would be sent to disturbed areas while landlords organized their more obedient tenants vigilante-style to deal with the neighborhood's agrarian rebels.

The Rebellion of 1798 and the subsequent union of the British and Irish parliaments two years later marks a watershed in Irish history. For more than a century thereafter, the viceroy (i.e., the lord lieutenant of Ireland) and law courts held sway in Dublin, but many of the policy decisions concerning the nation lay in the hands of an Irish secretary, associated with the British cabinet, who sat in the united parliament at West Minster. He was assisted by an under-secretary, permanently resident in Ireland. The relative influence of the viceroy, secretary and under-secretary at any given time depended on their drive and energy.

In 1812 Robert Peel, then a young and aspiring English Tory politician, became Irish secretary. Since it was wartime, most of the police work fell to the enlarged Irish garrison of about fifty thousand men. Due to the fact that they were already on the budget, their use in this role involved no cost to local government which was under the control of a magistracy who still had at their disposal an unimpressive force of watchmen-level Baronial Police. But again, when serious trouble arose, the assembled magistrates customarily requested the Irish executive in Dublin Castle ("the Castle") to "proclaim" a disturbed locality and send the troops. A proclamation constituted a modified version of martial law, and derived its legality from Insurrection Acts periodically renewed by the parliament of the United Kingdom. Insurrection Acts, which usually remained in force for several years, made for embarrassment in the British cabinet because political opponents cited them variously as evidence of oppression or a loss of control in Ireland.

Peel realized that the proclamation-plus-troops approach must come to an end when the Irish garrison returned to its normal strength of approximately twenty thousand at the close of the war. Some alternative would have to be found to prevent the secret societies' take-over of a great part of the police power in the countryside. One possible solution Peel ruled out: the use of the volunteer militia known as the Yeomanry. This force had been raised in 1796 to deal with the threat of rebellion, all but a few of its members being Protestant and most of them members of fraternal societies called Orange Lodges dedicated to the maintenance of Protestant supremacy. Employment of the Yeomanry remained a last resort, with the disadvantage of arming one section of the population against the other along sectarian lines.

Yet the idea of a large, professional police force of any kind was still publicly unacceptable. After some deliberation Peel as a move in the direction of professionalization decided on authorizing the organization of special bodies of "outrage specialists," perhaps roughly comparable in modern terms to special weapons assault teams ("S.W.A.T." squads) though the latter are primarily urban in focus. Such rural counter-terrorist forces were intended to be raised as necessity arose, placed under a stipendiary magistrate (i.e., a justice of the peace paid by the Castle), and sent where needed. The ideal recruit for this Peace Preservation Force, as it was called, would be a sergeant in the cavalry. In the proclaimed areas the stipendiary magistrate took official precedence over all the local unpaid magistrates, while his force remained on the scene until the disturbances ceased. The full cost of their presence was at first paid by the district, but later adjustments shared this responsibility with the Castle. The pay even for ordinary constables would be high, £50 per year, about the same as the London police.

Peel understood that the local magistrates were not effective agents of law and order, but at the same time had to face the reality of their political influence. The idea behind sending in a special force was that the demands of its upkeep should be an incentive for lax magistrates to do their duty, and that even the peasantry would cooperate with authorities to avoid added financial burdens. Under the scheme as it was ultimately passed, the viceroy could if he chose impose the force in a disturbed area, without invitation from the local magistrates. Cost for a year's upkeep of a contingent of the new body in a half-barony could be as expensive as £3,500 but the old ineffective Baronial Police continued to exist, and local magistrates at quarter sessions still had the power to appoint unpaid special constables.

In 1814, as the Irish garrison underwent a partial reduction to thirty thousand men, the Peace Preservation Force first went into action in Tipperary, when twenty former cavalry sergeants were sworn in under a stipendiary magistrate named Richard Willcocks. They arrived at a time when disturbances were quietening down and enjoyed apparent success, apart from being attacked as a patronage scheme in parliament. But as winter approached so did an agrarian crime wave which the police were at first unable to control. It would appear that if given time the force could be effective, especially under vigorous men like Willcocks, though local magistrates still hoped for a return to the old system of calling in troops under the Insurrection Act. But by its very nature the Peace Preservation Force was temporary, a response to local emergency, hence there could be no question of crime prevention through long-term patrol. As matters developed, the institution was useful as an experimental supplement to, though not the hoped for replacement of, the military who continued in a police role in spite of their reduced numbers, still acting under the Insurrection Act.

Committed to finding a solution and painfully aware of the limitations of the Peace Preservation Force, Peel was finally driven to the conclusion that nothing short of a Castle-controlled (i.e., centrally-controlled) permanent force covering all counties could effectively supplant the army's police function. In 1818 he resigned as chief secretary for Ireland, a somewhat disappointed yet still determined man who would have to face the problem of Ireland again when he became home secretary in 1822. By that time the breakdown of law and order in that country made the idea of a general, national police force more acceptable to the United Kingdom parliament.

In 1818 the new Irish secretary, Sir Charles Grant, a Scot, took office under the handicap of being at odds with the home secretary, Lord Sidmouth; the viceroy, Lord Talbot; and the under-secretary, William Gregory, on the highly contentious Catholic question. Grant, a comparatively liberal Tory, favoured the removal of remaining Catholic civil disabilities, whereas Sidmouth, Talbot and Gregory sided with the Ultra-Tories who opposed changes in Britain and Ireland alike to what was popularly termed the Protestant constitution in church and state. Moreover, Grant's attempt in 1819 to reduce the Irish garrison to seventeen thousand met rejection by the Ultra-Tory Duke of York, then in command of the army throughout the United Kingdom.

Grant, quite correctly, allowed no credence to widespread rumours that there existed subversive connections between contemporary British political Radicalism and rural unrest in Ireland. There was no such conspiracy, but given the desperate condition of the Irish peasantry none was necessary. Secret societies called Ribbonmen raided in nearly half the island during the winter of 1819-1820 and, with the garrison diminished, recourse followed to twelve hundred Yeomanry in Ulster, called out to release regular troops for service in the south. This move, which provided a stimulus to the dormant Orange Lodges, came in conjunction with the formation of some three thousand able-bodied army pensioners into auxiliary military units. Grant maintained that the presence of troops encouraged rather than inhibited rebellion, and he refused reinforcements from England while putting his faith in the Peace Preservation Force. But the latter remained essentially a series of independent *ad hoc* units with no reserves, as the military resources reasonably available to the Castle were already fully employed. Extensive delays developed in supplying proclaimed areas with the promised Peace Preservation Force contingents, and this in turn resulted in local magistrates' making renewed protests about their need for the traditional security of the Insurrection Act and troops.

As usual relative tranquility returned with the spring, and no immediate action was taken. Altogether over a thousand members of the Peace Preservation Force, eight hundred foot and two hundred and fifty mounted, had been dispatched to disturbed areas along with over six thousand military. Like Peel, Grant now began to think in terms of creating a permanent, national police, but his plans never matured. There were the usual local disorders and rumours of conspiracy during the winter of 1820-1821, yet nothing sufficient to shake up the government disposition to inaction. Moreover, the general good will which prevailed during the visit of King George IV to Ireland in the summer of 1821 could be taken as a favourable omen.

Nevertheless, trouble reappeared in October and it again became necessary to request military aid from England. With British army strength throughout the empire reduced by economy measures, the total number of troops in Ireland barely reached sixteen thousand. In view of the difficulties of external reinforcement, resort was had to the internal expedient of once more calling out the Yeomanry, this time in Dublin as well as the north, thus further encouraging an Orange revival already in progress. Meanwhile, Orangemen found their way into the Peace Preservation Force, doing nothing to lessen the denominational factor in the problem of law and order. Difficulties with recruiting and a decline in discipline and sectarian impartiality signalled a general unpopularity which by 1821 reached the point where even the government could no longer argue that the Peace Preservation Force constituted an adequate means of dealing with rural disorder. Conditions in Ireland assumed crisis proportions, and Talbot, the lord lieutenant, and Grant, the chief secretary, were both recalled.

Some degree of social (though not much political) harmony momentarily returned with the arrival of Lord Wellesley, the elder brother of the Duke of Wellington and likewise Irish-born, as viceroy in 1822. Wellesley was, in common with Grant, among those Tories who favoured Catholic emancipation (i.e., the restoration of the right of Catholics to sit in parliament), but he held no mandate to prepare the way for it during his service in Ireland. He soon undertook, however, and for the most part accomplished, the purging of the Castle administration of Orange influence. This though Henry Goulburn, the chief secretary for Ireland, and Peel, now home secretary, as yet remained political "Protestants," but there were limits to their effect on Irish policy. Prime Minister Lord Liverpool, in power since 1812, continued to personally be guardedly neutral on Catholic emancipation which remained an "open" question in a Tory cabinet openly divided on the issue.

Wellesley excluded use of the heavily Orange Yeomanry, and dismissed from office Irish Attorney General William Saurin, a former Orangeman of Huguenot descent. He found himself faced with a brief Orange "revolt" which amounted to no more than a few demonstrations, but it convinced Daniel O'Connell, an eminent Dublin lawyer, that the time had come to launch a legal Catholic mass movement — the Catholic Association — which employed the same means used by British political Radicals, particularly mass petitions and monster public meetings. Such tactics had recently failed in England but O'Connell, by insisting on sticking to a single issue (the Catholic right to again sit in parliament), won the active support of the Catholic church hierarchy. The financial resources of the movement were thus ensured, as the clergy collected "Catholic rent," a penny a month minimum per parishioner, at the church doors. It took over a year to make the association formidable, but O'Connell's powers as an orator and the excitement of legal mass demonstrations proved more attractive to most of the Catholic peasantry than did secret society criminal activity. Membership in O'Connell's organization was in any case less dangerous and appealed to those living in an urban as well as a rural environment, while secret societies were almost entirely restricted to alienated elements amongst the peasantry. There remained withal a hard core of embittered, violent men, usually but not exclusively Catholic, for whom secret societies were a way of life.

The emergence of the Catholic Association was roughly contemporary with the organization of the County Constabulary system by Wellesley. Created by the Irish Constabulary Act of 1822, Wellesley's County Police represented a marked advance in the chequered process of institutional development which ultimately issued in the Royal Irish Constabulary. New initiatives were in order as agrarian troubles renewed and much of the province of Munster slid into chaos with the same threatening in other areas. The Irish government asked for and received not only a customary Insurrection Act renewal, but the more radical step of the suspension of *habeas corpus*. However, the reduced garrison made it impossible to supply sufficient troops to hold down enough disturbed districts even with the benefit of this special legislation. The spectre of famine temporarily quieted the countryside in May, but once again the creation of a comprehensive police system covering all counties appeared to be the only alternative to increasing the garrison and living with a more or less permanent Insurrection Act, or accepting secret society domination over large sections of rural Ireland.

In response, the original Irish Constabulary Bill as sponsored by Wellesley intended to place a Castle-directed force in every one of the two hundred and fifty baronies, abolishing the old and inefficient Baronial Police while retaining the Peace Preservation Force for especially drastic situations. At the second reading local magistrates gained the power of appointing constables and sub-constables, sixteen to each barony, thus increasing the range of patronage. All personnel were to be under a chief constable nominated by the lord lieutenant, and provided with a house and paid £100 per year. The annual salary of constables and sub-constables was set at not more than £30, less than the London police, but prices in Ireland were low. A residence requirement existed in the area where the men were assigned, and they could take no other kind of work. Four inspectors paid £500 a year, one inspector for each province, held the power to discipline and if necessary dismiss unsatisfactory constables under the terms of the act.

Established immediately in fourteen counties where the need seemed greatest, Wellesley's County Constabulary received their weapons, equipment and houses from the Irish government. At the same time stipendiary magistrates, paid £500 *per annum*, were sent into areas where the local magistrates were non-resident, and provided with living quarters. Such resident, stipendiary magistrates, like those sanctioned by the earlier establishment of the Peace Preservation Force, held seniority over their local unpaid fellows on the bench. The Irish government undertook the initial financing of the County Constabulary, but included the stipulation that the counties would later be required to repay half the cost of the force's main-tenance. While representing progress, the Irish Constabulary Act and the force created by it still suffered the limitations of another com-promise imposed by the political influence of landowning local jus-tices of the peace whose support remained indispensible to the gov-ernment. Despite perennial talk of "reforming" the Irish magistracy, very few of its members found themselves removed from office.

Drunkenness on duty proved a problem, as it was to do in the case of the London Metropolitan Police, but only ten per cent of the County Constabulary were dismissed during the first two years. A new and fairly effective force appeared on the scene, though such effectiveness had to be measured against the self-disciplined mass movement led by Daniel O'Connell, which in a sense became a tacit partner in the exercise of police power. The O'Connellite leadership nonetheless publicly labelled the new County Constabulary a politically and religiously partisan body, and there was truth in this to the extent that in the early years Catholics made up less than a third of the membership. Yet it in no sense constituted an Orange force as it was unpopular with Ulster Protestants, one of the chief constables (himself a Protestant) being abused as "Papist Duff." By 1825, with four county inspectors installed, membership numbered four thousand five hundred, the Irish military garrison having again risen to twenty thousand men.

A relative peacefulness rare in living memory prevailed in Ireland, contemporary with the organization of both the County Constabulary and the Catholic Association. The Castle authorities accordingly questioned whether this happier state of affairs owed more to O'Connell's new-found moderating influence, or to the police. Some credit must in any case be allowed the constabulary, for without them the administration would have had little choice but to employ the Yeomanry. Attacks by the latter on even orderly demon-strations must have resulted sooner or later — probably sooner — and under these conditions O'Connell could hardly retain control of his followers. Unlike the Chartist leader Francis Place in England, however, O'Connell gave no credit to the police for the progress of his movement. Indeed much of his popularity depended upon his continual denunciation of the police as instruments of Orange repres-sion. But he nevertheless should have recognized that as they operated under Castle discipline they made no spontaneous attacks on his followers, while the alternative was the uncontrollable Yeomanry. For all his considerable talents as a reformer and gifted demagogue, O'Connell owed more to police assistance than he cared to admit or perhaps even understood. Indeed the Catholic Association anticipated in some respects the peaceful mass agitation directed by Mahatma Ghandi and Martin Luther King in other common law jurisdictions, not least in that Ghandi also worked within the framework of an established police system, and the success of the King movement depended much upon the protection of law enforcement officers.

The endemic yet localized secret society violence to persons, property and livestock which threatened government control of the countryside could not acquire central leadership or serious revolutionary purpose. If it had, it merely would have again invited massive military intervention. O'Connell's popular influence relied heavily on clerical support and a pre-condition of this, especially amongst the church hierarchy, was the rejection of illegal action. All this took time to become evident to the Castle, however, and much speculation at first ensued as to the revolutionary potential of the Catholic Association. It gradually became apparent that the organization intended to remain unarmed, while the admittedly impressive discipline it successfully imposed for mass meetings made a doubtful preparation for the battlefield. The real danger then emerged in the likelihood that the rise of O'Connell's movement would in turn encourage the Orange revival and, in the way of things in Ireland, lead to a major clash between the Orange and the Green.

To meet this danger, the government 1n 1825 passed legislation dissolving both the Catholic Association and the Orange Lodges for three years. In response O'Connell and his followers adroitly used legal stratagems to change their name and continued to function as before. As it turned out, the Orange Lodges were unable to do the same, being fraternal societies rooted in tradition and employing regalia and secret passwords. Above all they considered themselves supporters of the established order and many if not most of their leaders held government office of some kind at the county or local, though under Wellesley no longer at the Castle, level. In effect the act of 1825 broke the unity of the Orange movement while leaving that of the Green intact.

O'Connell took advantage of this in the general election of 1826, during which Irish Catholic tenants, ignoring the wishes of most Protestant landlords, voted *en masse* for those Protestant candidates who favoured Catholic emancipation. At the same juncture the British electorate returned a strong "Protestant" majority, for the time-being more than counter-balancing the increased Irish pro-emancipation contingent in the House of Commons. Immediate government concession was impossible but with Catholic emancipation plainly threatening, it appeared that the only recourse of the Protestant landlords would be a strong alliance with their militant co-religionist tenants. Some gestures were made in this direction by the organization of a loose network of Brunswick Constitutional Clubs. The latter Protestant organizations imitated the Catholic Association rather than the Orange Lodges in that their character was purely political, with no oaths, passwords, regalia or elaborate ceremonies involved.

At the end of 1827 Wellesley's replacement, Lord Anglesey, arrived. A veteran of Waterloo and in theory a political "Protestant," Anglesey in the summer of 1828 faced the crisis caused by the County Clare by-election in which O'Connell, having manifested his formidable influence with the Catholic electorate two years earlier, resolved to force the issue and run as a candidate although as a Catholic still ineligible to take a seat in parliament. He won easily against Vesey Fitzgerald, a Protestant advocate of emancipation, but in doing so unintentionally further stimulated Orangeism and its Brunswick Club allies. O'Connell, elated by the County Clare victory, decided that the next obvious step should be to further demonstrate the presumed impotence of Catholic emancipation's opponents by organizing a peaceful march through Ulster, the Protestant heartland.

O'Connell selected as the leader for this dangerous act of folly a liberal journalist, John ("Honest Jack") Lawless, who duly gathered a force of about ten thousand at the border city of Drogheda. Once in Orange territory attacks predictably started, two of Lawless' followers being killed and others injured. By the time it reached the city of Armagh the procession found itself confronted by thousands of armed Orangemen, for the most part apparently equipped with Yeomanry weapons which they had either never relinquished after service, or had acquired more informally. The local military commander, General Thornton, informed the chief secretary on 8 September that with only a hundred soldiers immediately available at the scene he could do nothing but try to act as a mediator between the two groups. At this point O'Connell responsibly prevented further bloodshed by calling off the Lawless campaign, having demonstrated not as he hoped the weakness of Orangeism, but its continued vitality. He had at the same time, however, also advertised the limits of government police power.

For O'Connell the Lawless episode represented merely a temporary defeat, and that more apparent than real. Wellington, Tory prime minister since early in 1828, and Peel, the home secretary and leader in the Commons, after the Ulster march came to the reluctant conclusion (though for months only privately) that further resistance to Catholic emancipation was futile. The only alternative, massive military re-intervention and perhaps civil war in Ireland on the scale of 1798, they rejected as politically now unacceptable if not impossible. In the new parliamentary session of 1829 they passed Catholic emancipation as a government measure with Whig and Radical support, but only after an exceedingly bitter struggle within the Tory party. The die-hard Ultra-Tories and the king attempted to resist, shocked at what they considered the betrayal of the Protestant constitution in church and state by Wellington and Peel, heretofore two of its most prominent supporters. Though strong in the Lords and with much British and Irish Protestant popular sentiment on their side against Catholic emancipation, the Ultras could find no sufficiently effective leader in the lower house. They accordingly failed in their efforts to form a new government, the king retained the Wellington and Peel administration in office, and O'Connell and his co-religionists took their seats in parliament.

The more enthusiastic proponents of Catholic emancipation claimed that passage of the measure would, if not settle all Irish problems, at least produce a temporary quiet in the nation and a belief in the promise of better times. In effect it merely dissolved the Catholic Association, and with it O'Connell's ability to offer an attractive alternative to secret society violence. Moreover the hundred thousand or so forty shilling freeholders who constituted the source of O'Connell's voting strength were disfranchised at the same time as emancipation, the new property qualification reducing the number of voting Irish freeholders to sixty thousand. Many problems and grievances remained, prominent among them the legal obligation of all citizens to pay tithe and cess to the established Protestant (Anglican) Church of Ireland, whether or not they were members. The resentment of Presbyterians and other Protestant non-Anglicans at this requirement was more than shared by the Catholic community, for whom the sense of injustice in this as in several other particulars made quiet for long impossible.

With much of O'Connell's influence gone and renewed secret society violence being answered by Orange retaliation, some elements among the clergy, hoping to secure a return to peaceful protest around an issue appealing to Catholics, set off what became known as the Tithe War. Resistance to the tithe was in fact a step away from mere demonstration, to civil disobedience. Failure to pay tithe normally led to the seizure of livestock though the vagaries of the law were such that this could not be done if it involved breaking a lock, nor could animals be taken between sunset and dawn. As resistance to tithe collection increased, secret societies became involved, and by 1830 law and order had sunk to the level of 1820.

This resulted in reactivation of the Yeomanry, reinforcement of the garrison and the deployment of over 1200 members of the Peace Preservation Force since the County Constabulary, though steadily growing in numbers and efficiency, could not alone control such a situation as the Tithe War produced. Efforts had indeed been made to relieve the County Constabulary of the more unpopular aspects of law enforcement. Castle policy avoided their employment as bailiffs in the collection of rents, as fish and game law enforcement officers, as toll-collectors, and as assistants to landlords in the eviction of tenants. Further, no serious attempt was made to employ police in tithe collection until 1832. The County Constabulary increased from about four thousand eight hundred in 1824 to six thousand in 1830. Though when necessary assisted by the military and the Peace Preservation Force, and less frequently by several thousand activated military pensioners, they still constituted the main, regular police arm of the Castle.

In matters of police reform the Whig government which took office late in 1830 enjoyed a strong position inasmuch as their Tory predecessors, and Peel in particular, could not logically oppose measures which they had formerly advocated. After 1828 sub-inspectors were assigned to each county, facilitating the elimination of inefficient political appointments. By 1833 permanent stipendiary magistrates served two-thirds of the counties and four counties not so circumstanced still benefitted from temporary stipendiaries provided by the Peace Preservation Force. In the same year the Whig administration, sensitive to the charge of an Orange police force, exerted itself to employ Catholics in the County Constabulary and ordinary magistrates ceased altogether to make nominations to the lower ranks. Most of the newly appointed constables were young and, in what was to be an on-going policy, the aim was to reduce the number of married men in the force to twenty per cent. Few Catholics staffed the higher ranks, but in 1834 they numbered about a third of the total personnel. Some parallels exist between efforts to recruit black police in American cities after the 1960s, and the recruitment of Catholics to the County Constabulary and its Irish and Royal Irish Constabulary successors, the ideal being an impartial force which held the respect of all sections of the community.

An important step toward the creation of such an institution was taken by Irish Under-Secretary Thomas Drummond. An engineer by training and a reformer in political sympathies, 37 years of age at the time of his taking office, Drummond was largely responsible for the Constabulary Act of 1836. The latter transformed the County Constabulary into the Irish Constabulary and brought the force under *de jure* as well as *de facto* Castle control through the appointment of Colonel James Shaw-Kennedy to the newly created position of inspector-general. Shaw-Kennedy, a non-political soldier whom Peel had originally offered the post given Sir Charles Rowan in the London Metropolitan Police, proved an excellent choice.

In the transition from County to Irish Constabulary, change occurred mostly at the top. The vast majority of the seven thousand four hundred constables continued to serve with the usual turn-over rate of about ten per cent a year. The Irish Constabulary incorporated the six hundred active members of the Peace Preservation Force, and henceforth there existed no civil "S.W.A.T." squads though the army remained a last resort in severe emergencies. The Constabulary Act of 1836 established two classes of sub-constable, the higher paid £27 14 shillings and the lower £24 *per annum*. This represented a thirteen per cent wage increase but remained low in comparison to the £50 paid a London constable. Nonetheless it was high by Irish standards, about twice that of a casual labourer. Full constables in the Irish Constabulary earned £32 7 shillings a year. Three years later these wage rates were slightly reduced, but few resignations resulted. As in the County Constabulary, marriage was discouraged, the aim still being to keep married personnel to no more than twenty per cent of the force. Men could be transferred from one county to another, and transfer became a means of removing unpopular constables from a dangerous environment as well as providing a second chance for those who had made serious mistakes.

Promotion from the Irish Constabulary ranks rarely went beyond the rank of head constable, a kind of senior non-commissioned officer. In the first few years recruiting at the officer level was normally from the army, but those entering the force would have to start at the lowest commissioned rank. By this means it was assumed that outsiders would not be appointed over the heads of the established hierarchy. In 1839 an Irish Constabulary depot opened at Phoenix Park in Dublin. By 1842 officer cadets trained there in a special school after which they would be examined not only in routine police matters, but also with regard to their degree of literacy. Cadets while training received a constable's pay, and on completion of the course entered the force with the rank of sub-inspector third class.

The Irish Constabulary was supposed to be politically and religiously non-partisan, but Drummond considered it too Tory for his taste as it stood in 1836. Accordingly, Whig connections for a time proved an advantage for aspiring candidates and, as it was believed that constabulary officers would have to get along with the gentry, preference was given to sons of that class. Yet the ranks were not neglected: after 1839 one out of every three promotions had to be from the ranks. At the same time preference was given to the sons of serving officers. Inspector-General Shaw-Kennedy wanted a completely non-political force but found his recommendations for promotion to senior officer rejected in favour of those with political influence, though there was no tolerance of incompetence. In any case he made his point by resigning in 1838, after which his successor, Colonel Duncan McGregor, was given total control of appointments.

Thomas Drummond's role in police reform has sometimes been over-estimated, but he remains an undoubtedly forceful personality who appeared on the scene as under-secretary at a time when change was in the air. He took charge of that which his predecessors had planned and in some cases already introduced, and gave it a reality and a permanence which had not hitherto been possible. Not least, during his term in office the fast-ebbing prejudicial influence of local magistrates on police arrangements came to an end. By degrees all categories of crime, including the secret society variety, subsided as the Irish Constabulary made its presence felt in the countryside. However secret society influence remained, sustained by the general sympathy of the people, and there developed no parallel of the Irish force gaining the kind of popularity enjoyed by the London Metropolitan Police.

After taking his seat in parliament, O'Connell remained in opposition until 1835 when he began trading Irish support in the Commons for concessions from the Whig government. With the coming of the Conservatives to power 1n 1841 he resumed an opposition stance, commencing a campaign for the repeal of the 1800 Act of Union of the British and Irish parliaments. Like his Catholic emancipation movement in the 1820s, the intention was to stay within the law, agitating principally by petitions and legal mass demonstrations. He found the ground well-prepared by popular resistance to the New Poor Law, extended to Ireland by the Whigs in 1838, which called for segregation of the able-bodied poor in poor houses sustained by local rate-payers. The police were already in difficulties trying to enforce so widely condemned a law, when O'Connell opened his repeal of the union campaign in 1843.

Peel, then prime minister, let the mass meetings proceed, with the police merely collecting information, but at the same time he increased the strength of the British garrison. In the course of agitation O'Connell was arrested for sedition, though no conviction resulted. Within a few years the repeal movement found itself overtaken by the massive tragedy of the potato blight and consequent Irish famine which began in 1846. Meanwhile, however, a younger generation of journalists gathered around *The Nation*, a nationalist newspaper, began to challenge O'Connell's leadership.

The year 1848 began with a successful revolution in France and was marked by liberal-nationalist revolutions nearly everywhere in central Europe which resulted in a temporary suspension of authority but ultimately failed. In Britain, as noted, the Chartist mass demonstrations fizzled out when confronted by the even more numerous special constables. Yet under existing conditions in Ireland a revolt of some dimension could be expected, and young journalists who had broken with O'Connell attempted to lead it. They possessed no experience in conspiracy and, perhaps more curiously, no social programme. Yet they were idealists who, forgetting 1798 and many other bloody chapters in British-Irish relations, anticipated a rather gentlemanly affair in which there would be no looting, or the abuse or murder of non combatants. Further, they believed a spontaneous successful rising could be produced through the diffusion of military knowledge in the press. The death of O'Connell while on a pilgrimage to Rome in 1847 left the constitutionalist Irish nationalists temporarily without a leader, so that it fell to the Catholic clergy to put on the brakes. This they determined to do because of the apparent association of the Young Irelanders, as the revolutionaries called themselves, with Continental liberal anti-clericalism .

The Young Irelanders were in no sense professional revolutionaries, all being capable, as they later proved, of making careers along more orthodox professional lines. The oldest, William Smith O'Brien, was thirty-five, a Protestant from an aristocratic family. They sought support from the newly-founded French Republic, but received no encouragement as the French government was anxious for good relations with Britain. The police took the initiative by arresting seven key leaders including Gavan Duffy, a prominent Radical journalist. Four, Duffy among them, were held in custody. Three, including Thomas D'Arcy Magee, a future father of Canadian Confederation, cabinet minister, and victim of Fenian assassination in Ottawa, were released on bail. A Coercion Act took effect in three counties in 1848, *habeas corpus* being suspended for seven months throughout the nation. The Irish garrison now stood at twenty-nine thousand with eleven thousand concentrated in Dublin; the constabulary numbered by this time numbered over twelve thousand men.

Only a tiny part of the dreamed of nationalist army actually turned out, very few carrying arms. Appeals to the police and British forces to "come over" made no headway, and as the Rebels marched about the countryside they found their band of several hundred melting away while priests quietly encouraged their members to abandon the project. Violence of sorts came at Ballingarry in County Tipperary, where forty-six constables took refuge in a farmhouse, besieged by a crowd of three thousand. Upon stones being thrown at the house, the police opened fire, killing two. Smith O'Brien attempted to negotiate at the scene as his followers faded away, the remainder dispersing with the arrival of a detachment of thirty-four more constables. The subsequently exiled leaders mostly went on to make successful careers abroad, and no executions ensued from the attempted Young Ireland rising. The latter over, the Irish Constabulary resumed routine duties which included such pedestrian matters as census-taking and collecting agricultural statistics.

A decade passed before a new revolutionary threat arose, this time inspired, and in theory supported, by Irish Americans. James Stephens planned to organize an underground movement led by professional soldiers and financed by the Irish in the United States. Stephens, who took pride in his role as a professional revolutionary, was in the late 1850s and early 1860s able to get a large number of the more nationalistic of his countrymen in Ireland to take the secret oath of his organization named the Fenian Brotherhood, but as long as he retained leadership he never considered the time ripe for rebellion in his homeland. Further, before long he quarrelled with the American Fenians who in turn divided on the question of invading Canada. This a substantial faction of them attempted in 1866 and again in 1870, but that story belongs to Canadian rather than Irish history.

With the Fenian Brotherhood thus split, Stephens found himself in effect deposed by his former followers. Leadership of the Fenian wing which favoured immediate revolt in Ireland fell to Irish American veterans of the U.S. Civil War accustomed to battle, and impatient to act. They possessed audacity but not much else, proving themselves incapable of organizing a general uprising. They demonstrated, however, considerable capacity for guerilla-style action which, given the element of surprise, could have its effect. Yet surprise always remained difficult to achieve because the Fenian movement was riddled with informers. Plans nevertheless went ahead and an intended rebellion commenced on the 3rd of March 1867 when several thousand Fenians gathered outside Dublin seized two police barracks, but then dispersed with the arrival of troops. Similar half-hearted, tentative risings occurred in Counties Tipperary, Limerick, Clare, Queen's and Louth. There again, few who turned out were armed and the would-be insurgents lacked trained officers to effectively lead them. Within six days it was all over, with most of such leadership as existed in custody or, like the Young Irelanders before them, going into exile.

Fenian activities in England, as stated previously, spurred the creation of the Special Branch which had intelligence links to the Irish Constabulary though not directly concerned with its daily routine. The most important effect of the attempted Fenian rising of 1867 on the Irish Constabulary was the award of the designation "Royal" in recognition of services rendered on that and other occasions. The Royal Irish Constabulary (henceforth widely known by their R.I.C. acronym), though never popular, for another decade and more held control of the countryside as the crime rate fell and secret society activity declined in spite of prompting from the remnants of the Fenians in America. This took a serious terrorist turn in 1884 with the so-called Dynamite War involving bombing in London, which led for a time to the suspension of *habeas corpus* there. Meanwhile in Ireland itself the Home Rule movement, started in 1870, gained a dynamic leader in Charles Stewart Parnell, like Smith O'Brien a Protestant and a strong nationalist. Parnell, following in O'Connell's steps, founded a parliamentary party linked to mass organization, combining opposition politics at Westminster with militant social action in Ireland.

Such social action notably meant resistance to evictions of tenants for non-payment of rent, and thus confrontation with the police and military who in enforcing the law had the rather thankless task of supporting landlords against tenants. By 1882 there were five thousand evictions annually, the main responsibility for them resting with the eighty-one resident magistrates sustained as a matter of course by about fourteen thousand five hundred Royal Irish Constabulary and, when necessary, thirty thousand troops. The crime branch of the R.I.C. and the G Section of the Dublin Metropolitan Police — the latter unarmed, organized on the

London model — regularly supplied intelligence. Police informers reported that no immediate plans existed for another general uprising, but they could not guarantee there would not be isolated acts of terrorism. The most spectacular of these was doubtless the murder of Chief Secretary Lord Frederick Cavendish, and Under-Secretary Thomas Burke, in Phoenix Park on 6 May 1882 by a small group calling themselves the Invincibles.

The Phoenix Park killings, roughly contemporary with the Dynamite War's bombing campaign in England, made clear the necessity of bringing the investigation of political crime under a centralized agency. Since the advent of Fenianism some R.I.C. men had been stationed in English cities which possessed a large Irish population. There were sixteen such individuals in 1883, five of them in London. The same year the obviously increased efficiency to be attained by placing these men and the entire responsibility for political intelligence and investigation under the home office resulted in the creation of the Special Branch.

Meanwhile, with the growing popular and parliamentary strength of Parnell and his lieutenant Michael Davitt, even Irish Americans shifted their support to the moral force movement. This by no means left police with a trouble-free control of the countryside, however, and incidents still occurred like that at Mitchelstown, County Cork, on 9 September 1887. There a heavily outnumbered R.I.C. detachment fired on a mob and killed two. Yet in most cases crowd control even under very trying circumstances was maintained by constables using batons, and there were few serious casualties. By the turn of the century the Royal Irish Constabulary was a famous, respected, if far from popular force. As Home Rule appeared ever more clearly on the political horizon after 1905, indeed as a policy of the Liberal government, the R.I.C.'s days appeared to be numbered, and so they were. Yet it was perhaps fitting that a force born amid violence should go out with a bang and not a whimper, as proved to be the case.

Under threat of organized, armed Protestant resistance in Ulster, the British government by 1914 was prepared to at least temporarily give the province a special status separate from a Home Rule regime in the rest of Ireland. But the majority of Home Rulers rejected such a partition, and there the matter rested with Home Rule postponed for the duration of World War I. The Irish War of Independence, begun in 1920, waged against the British by the Irish Republican Army (I.R.A.), was probably unnecessary as what was gained — *de facto* independence minus the six counties of Ulster — had already been virtually conceded. However, doubts about the sincerity of the government headed by David Lloyd George provided an opening for the physical force wing of the independence movement.

At this point the ranks of the R.I.C. had been depleted by military service in the just completed struggle with the Central Powers, and with its demise expected the morale of the force was low. Under these conditions it lost control of the countryside as isolated police posts were attacked and the families of constables endangered. Mass resignations resulted, leaving the British government with but two alternatives short of unconditional surrender to rebellion: reinforcing the police or making a massive military intervention. The choice of the former course led to the force being built up by enlisting restless unemployed or under-employed veterans in Britain. But, as Richard Bennett rightly states in his study of *The Black and Tans*, contrary to Irish nationalist folklore these volunteers were not "the sweepings of the English gaols," even though some of them under greater or lesser provocation certainly subsequently behaved like they were. Foremost, and in some quarters especially feared, amongst them featured the so-called officer cadets of the R.I.C. Auxiliary Division, recruited from former British army combat officers, paid £1 a day and organized in companies of a hundred as special strike forces or shock troops bearing some resemblance to Peel's Peace Preservation Force in the previous century.

With not enough complete Royal Irish Constabulary uniforms to go around, the reinforcements made various motley improvisations combining dark green R.I.C. garb with army khaki and some, especially the Auxiliaries at the beginning, except in head gear wore full war surplus army service dress. The Auxiliaries later most commonly wore a dark blue police uniform, their original tam-o'-shanter bonnets replaced by an equally jaunty dark green balmoral likewise bearing the R.I.C. harp and crown insignia. In any case, supposedly because of the colour of their dress they and the other reinforcements of 1920-1921 collectively entered history as the Black and Tans (perhaps not altogether coincidentally also the name of a breed of hounds), though the classification arguably does not strictly apply to the Auxiliaries who, all being former officers, were recruited separately and operationally remained in units more or less distinct from other R.I.C. personnel.

It is virtually axiomatic that when a readily identifiable, regularly constituted (even if as in this instance somewhat irregularly uniformed) force mounts operations against un-uniformed partisans such as the I.R.A. Volunteers, the strong tendency on both sides will be to neglect the conventions of comparatively "civilized" engagement and descend to methods of increasingly promiscuous atrocity, terror and counter-terror, reprisal and counter-reprisal. In these circumstances non-combatants and the vulnerable frequently suffer as much or more than the "guilty," or those actively pursuing hostilities. For Ireland, such was the case in 1920-1921 as in 1798, each side paying the other in a sorry catalogue of arson and murder. Hence the rough and ready, at times flagrantly lawless, behaviour of numbers of the Black and Tans, and the Auxiliaries, toward an Irish Catholic population they considered hid un-uniformed killers in its midst and thus made itself deserving of being dealt with in brutal terms. Such conduct made them in turn easy targets for Irish nationalist propaganda, and their name soon became widely infamous. But for all that they proved an effective counter-guerilla force that wore down the I.R.A. to the point where the latter was willing to negotiate.

The new Irish Free State replaced the R.I.C. with the *Garda Siochana*, an unarmed police (except in the Ulster border areas) and a very different type of force. But in the six northern counties the R.I.C. survives as the Royal Ulster Constabulary, and there its battle with the I.R.A. continues. Although always a controversial force, the Royal Irish Constabulary possessed certain features which made it a model for rural police throughout the empire and then the commonwealth. It was a civil organization, yet armed and under military discipline, always ready to deal with armed opposition. At the same time it also performed mundane, civil service administrative functions like census-taking and collecting statistics which demanded a significant level of literacy. Basically, apart from the aberration of the Black and Tan period, R.I.C. personnel saw themselves not primarily as a fighting force but as keepers of the peace very much in the common law tradition.

CHAPTER VI

POLICE IN INDIA

POLICING THE INDIAN SUB-CONTINENT constituted the greatest administrative responsibility faced by the British Empire. Indigenous Indian police institutions were far in advance, in terms of sophistication of organization, of anything found in Britain at the time the East India Company became a real power on the scene, about 1765. No relevant British police experience existed to serve as a guide to policy.

In the first century and a half of the British presence in India (roughly 1600-1765) there were only three enclaves under East India Company control: Bombay, Calcutta, and Madras. Called presidencies, they bore some resemblance to later developments in Hong Kong and Singapore in that they were native-populated cities with a European administration. In the eighteenth century the East India Company by virtue of a charter from the British Crown exercised power over resident British citizens. In Calcutta and Madras the Indian population was governed by authority granted by the Moghul Emperor. Bombay, not part of the Moghul Empire, was governed entirely by the company. Such police arrangements as obtained in the presidencies were at first makeshift and rudimentary, usually carried out by a military battalion composed of an ethnically mixed lot of Europeans, Eurasians and native Indians loosely referred to as the militia.

On the other hand, professional police, or at least officials assigned to police duties, seem to have been in existence as early as

300 B.C. A highly developed secret service system employing travelling merchants, holy men, and public entertainers provided information which today would be classified as police intelligence. The Hindu manual of statecraft, *The Arthastra* (ca. 700 A.D.), speaks of urban police centred around the *nagareska* who in later Muslim terms became known as the *kotwal*. The latter was a police official, the urban police stations being known as *kotwali*. The *kotwal* kept a list of substantial citizens obliged to take turns at patrol in their districts, much like the system introduced in eighteenth century New York City.

Though the active enforcement of his regulations had mostly ceased by the time the East India Company first became involved in India, the Moghul Emperor Akbar (1556-1605) established a police bureaucracy which in some respects went beyond even that of Oliver Cromwell's regime in Britain. Akbar decreed that:

> The *kotwals* of cities, towns, and villages, in conjunction with the royal clerks, shall prepare a register of the houses and buildings of the same, which register shall include a particular description of the inhabitants of each habitation. One house shall become security for another; so that they shall all be reciprocally pledged and bound each for the other. They shall be divided into districts, each having a chief or prefect, to whose superintendence the district shall be subject. Secret intelligencers or spies shall be appointed to each district, who shall keep a journal of local occurrences, arrivals, and departures, happening either by day or night. When any theft, fire, or other misfortune mayhappen, the neighbours shall render immediate assistance; especially the prefect and public informers, who, failing to attend on such occasions, unless unavoidably prevented, shall be held responsible for the omission. No person shall be permitted to travel beyond, or to arrive within, the limits of the district, without the knowledge of the prefect, the neighbours, or public informers. Those who cannot provide security shall reside in a separate place of abode, to be allotted to them by the prefect of the district and the public informers ...

The *kotwal*, whose position in some respects was roughly analogous to aspects of both an English magistrate and sheriff, held judicial powers, and was expected to attend at *durbar* when the local governor held court. In the countryside, where most of the people lived in villages, responsibility for law and order was in the hands of the *patel* or village headman, assisted by *chowkidars* or hereditary watchmen. As most moveable wealth consisted of livestock, the *chowkidars* acted as trackers who with the aid of their counterparts in neighbouring villages could trace the movement of stolen animals.

At a higher level the provincial governors of the Moghul Empire appointed *faujdals*, essentially revenue officers with administrative responsibilities which included policing. *Faujdals* in turn had the assistance of station officers known as *thanadars*. They themselves were mobile, seeing to highway patrol and in general moving about the country with armed escorts to "show the flag" of imperial authority. The *faujdals* functioned well enough until the early years of the eighteenth century when Moghul power began to dissolve and provincial governors, usually called *nizams*, were inclined to leave policing to *zemindars*, tax-farmers-cum-landlords.

In 1765 the East India Company became a *de jure* as well as *de facto* power when it took over the *dwani*, the right to collect taxes in Bengal. It was at first expected that the *dwani* would be a source of wealth, but in practice the costs of government which went with it brought the company to the verge of bankruptcy. This led the crown to appoint a governor general and council in 1773, with jurisdiction over the three presidencies. Warren Hastings, the first governor, who had also ruled under the company, left the *zemindars* in control of Bengal. His successor, Lord Cornwallis, perhaps most often remembered for his surrender at Yorktown, Virginia, in 1781, thought differently. He transferred police power to district officers generally known as collectors for their revenue responsibilities. After 1786 police, judicial and revenue powers were therefore all combined in the hands of the collectors who were in some sense the successors of the *faujdals*, but there still existed no counterpart of the *thanadar*. The introduction of the *darogha* system remedied this somewhat imperfectly in 1792. A *darogha* or station officer had charge of a district of roughly four hundred square miles. He held no judicial authority, and indeed no power to investigate, but could take evidence from witnesses. Village *chowkidars* or watchmen served under his authority, which was in turn sustained by a force of up to forty armed men recruited by the *darogha* personally. This body normally included several *jamadars* who acted as non-commissioned officers. When the judicial authority of the collector became a matter of debate, Cornwallis transferred it to a district judge. Yet this created difficulties, judicial power being returned to the collector in 1831 where it remained until the police reforms of 1862.

The first quarter of the nineteenth century saw the defeat of the Mahratta Confederation and the elimination of French influence, leaving the East India Company in virtual control of the sub-Continent. Such control was exercised either through the direct rule of the company in the much expanded presidencies, or indirectly through the states of the princes, which were in effect British protectorates. Needless to say, in these circumstances no uniform system of police existed. In Madras an hereditary police chief, the *pedda nark*, commanded a force of watchmen until 1806. After that a European chief was installed, supported by seven European constables and five hundred Indian police styled *peons*, the latter including eighty mounted men. Outside the city of Madras local chieftains known as *polygars* exercised police power until 1802, at which time it was transferred to the *zellahs* or Indian district judges before passing back to the collectors in 1816. There it remained until the police reforms of the 1850s. Bombay maintained a police battalion of forty-eight officers and four hundred men which patrolled the streets at night. A lieutenant of police was appointed in 1787 with the authority of a magistrate, which he retained but ceased to exercise when several police officers were appointed magistrates in 1816. This settled the matter of urban police for two generations, but nothing noteworthy was done about a rural force until the organization of the so-called *mofusil* (i.e., district) police in 1827. They included three elements: the village *chowkidar*, a paid district police, and a support group of several bodies of irregulars. Responsibility as in other provinces rested with the collector, who was assisted by *mamlatars* or paid subordinate revenue officers. The *mamlatars* each commanded a small force of *peons*, armed retainers, who performed police duties.

Some aspects of Indian society were unacceptable to the British conscience, but company officials long thought they had no power to change them. Foremost among these ranked the practice of *suttee*, or the burning alive of a widow on her husband's funeral pyre, a custom contrary to the precepts of Islam as well as Christianity but one with which the Moghul Emperor found it inexpedient to interfere. Earlier British governor generals like Lord Wellesley, elder brother of the Duke of Wellington, contemplated action against *suttee*, yet hesitated. It remained for Sir William Bentinck, a strong evangelical Christian who took office in 1829, to face up to the matter. When he did, protests for a time ensued, and isolated instances of armed resistance, but no threat of a general uprising. Bentinck was a governor general of moral courage, unwilling to tolerate the continuance of obvious evil, and prepared to take risks.

It soon became apparent to Bentinck that the diverse and changing police forces of the presidencies were incapable of effectively dealing with wandering bands of criminals known as *dacoits*, and certainly not with an hereditary secret society like the *thuggee* (from whence the word "thug" entered the English language) whose existence became known to the authorities about 1810. The origins of the *thuggee* (or *thugs*) remain a matter of controversy. They were a religious cult who worshipped Kali, the Hindu goddess of death. According to their view, they performed a divine mission to serve society by reducing the population, for which task they earned a just compensation by appropriating the property of their victims. Drawn from all parts of India, the thugs communicated amongst themselves in a patois unintelligible to outsiders. Their favourite technique was to gather in bands and move along the roads, stopping at fairs, markets and other public places to select likely victims. Usually one or two of their more presentable members would strike up an acquaintance with suitable strangers, and induce them to seek safety from the dangers of the road by joining their group of travellers. Then, when in a sufficiently remote location, the victims would be strangled with a knotted scarf, stripped of their belongings, and buried in a hidden grave.

Zemindars and village headmen did not usually interfere with thugs' activities, in some cases being bribed to look the other way. Bentinck accordingly, as well as suppressing *suttee*, moved in 1830 to give responsibility for the elimination of the *thug* problem to the very capable Captain William Sleeman, who became head of a unit devoted to the elimination of *dacoity* and *thuggee* in 1835. Sleeman was first named superintendent, then commissioner, of what was in practice a criminal investigation department. Attempts to break the *thugs* failed in the past because of the apparent impossibility of infiltrating an hereditary secret organization. Yet, on the other hand, few *thuggee* were fanatics with an ultimate commitment to the cult. Once arrested, many members readily confessed and implicated others in an effort to save their own lives. It proved a long, complicated task, but *thugs* who confessed led the police to the graves of victims and provided crucial evidence in court. Within five years three thousand six hundred and eighty-nine members of the murderous cult had been tried, with four hundred and sixty-six hanged, one thousand five hundred and sixty-four transported for life, and nine hundred and thirty-three given life sentences. With the *thug* terror broken, Sleeman's police turned their full attention to other varieties of criminals, particularly those engaged in *dacoity*. Sleeman's department functioned until the police reforms of 1862, whereupon it ceased to exist in British India but survived in some of the territories of the princes.

The three Presidencies of Bengal, Bombay and Calcutta were gradually expanded and supplemented by other provinces until there existed nine at the end of the century. One of the most dramatic incidents involved the acquisition of Sind, now part of West Pakistan. This was accomplished in 1847 by Sir Charles Napier, the former commander eight years earlier of the northern military district during the Chartist disturbances in England. Napier was an imaginative and efficient officer prepared to benefit by experience. He saw at once the limitations of purely military government and the *darogha* system which prevailed in Bengal. By the same token, Napier appears to have been among the first to consider the Irish Constabulary as a possible example for India, and indeed the organization was already beginning to acquire a positive reputation in imperial circles, having been in existence eleven years at the time of the conquest of Sind.

Napier appointed an inspector general of police for the province as well as a superintendent in each district, co-equal but subordinate to the collector. At this point Napier's police departed from the Irish model, being divided into urban, rural and mounted elements. In practice, urban police were armed and drilled infantry, but assigned to police duties. In the countryside foot constables served to guard prisoners, police posts and valuable goods in transit: that is to say, they were essentially security guards. Mounted patrols, who earned higher pay, supplemented these arrangements; and as the superintendents were European, the system ensured the presence of a senior ranking European police officer in each district. Apart from Sind, in 1853 the Bombay Presidency adopted the same system, replacing the existing police. In Madras reform came almost incidentally by way of the Torture Commission which investigated charges about the employment of torture in the collection of revenue. It discovered that this was rare in the revenue department, but more common in the obtaining of evidence needed for convictions in courts of law. Several years passed debating possible improvements in organization, until in 1859 authorities chose the Bombay system with an overall inspector general of police, and district superintendents subordinate to revenue officers.

In Bengal discussion of reform was interrupted by the revolt of the Bengal native army in 1857, initiating a bloody and dramatic series of events collectively known as the Indian Mutiny. As British rule was supported by a British-led but predominantly Indian army, the mutiny struck at the heart of imperial power. The uprising resulted in large part from the policy of pushing modernization without showing sufficient sensitivity towards Indian traditions and values, the spark which set it off being a rumour that the paper wrappings of cartridges for army service weapons — this at a time when the Model 1853 Enfield rifle was replacing the old Brown Bess musket — were being coated variously with beef or pork fat. To handle (much less bite, as required in the standard drill when charging muzzle-loading weapons with such a cartridge) an object coated with the proceeds of slaughtered swine was anathema to Muslims, the same being true with respect to cattle for Hindus.

Although it enjoyed widespread but by no means universal sympathy amongst the wider native Indian population, no general uprising occurred and the revolt remained confined to the Bengal army. After putting down the mutiny with prodigious feats of arms performed by sometimes vastly out-numbered British and loyal native troops, the imperial authorities in 1858 ended both the East India Company role and the facade of Moghul rule on the sub-Continent. Under the new system a secretary of state for India sat in the British cabinet, the resident governor general was styled the viceroy; and the army henceforth recruited mostly in the north, relying heavily on Sikhs and Gurkhas with their warrior traditions and military prowess which had impressed the British when they tested its mettle as opponents in past battles. The administration at the same time abandoned the policy of phasing out the states of the princes, placing more emphasis on courting them as allies. In matters of policing the princes would as a rule, after some delay and under the supervision of a British high commissioner, adopt a local version of the system which prevailed in territory under direct British jurisdiction.

Several years after the mutiny, a commission appointed to review the entire question of police in India submitted a report which resulted in the Police Act of 1861 whose provisions came into effect the following year. This brought about a uniform system for virtually all the provinces in which existing military police were disbanded, and the Irish model introduced everywhere with the exception of the Punjab frontier districts (later usually called the Northwest Frontier), where a constant military presence and tribal diplomacy were needed to maintain order. Police would have a uniform system, but be organized separately with an inspector general in each province. For the first two years an all-India inspector general held office, but the post was abolished on the grounds that it had no duties. A provincial inspector general could be drawn from serving police officers, but officialdom considered it better to appoint a man from some other branch of the civil service. Deputy inspector generals in charge of divisions within each province were to be appointed as needed.

Poona Mounted Police.

The higher ranks — inspector general, deputy inspector general, superintendent, and assistant superintendent — held commissions directly from the secretary of state for India in London, and were designated imperial police. For nearly a generation most of the occupants of these levels came from the army; then by appointment and examination; and still later by competitive examination. Promotion to the higher from lower ranks was rare, but after 1902 the post of deputy superintendent was created, being an officer usually appointed by the provincial government with the intention of rewarding the more able men at lower levels in the force. However, direct appointments as distinct from promotions could still be made to deputy superintendentships, below which there existed no uniformity in rank structure. For example there were six grades of inspectors in Bombay, three in Madras and four in Bengal. Under these grades there was the rank of sub-inspector; then that of the head constable, who wore three stripes like a sergeant; and finally the constable. Inspectors were normally promoted from the ranks but direct appointments could be made by superintendents. Constables were recruited locally when possible, though this proved difficult in areas with high wage scales. Pay differentials were extreme. A constable typically received about 8 rupees (rs) a month; a sub-inspector got 25 rs which increased to 50 rs for inspectors, while about 150 rs for the same period was the pay of assistant and deputy superintendents. Superintendents by the same token earned 500 rs. Total Indian police personnel numbered some one hundred and forty thousand with about fifteen thousand officers.

Unlike the practice in the Irish (after 1867 the Royal Irish) Constabulary, Indian police were divided into armed and unarmed sections, those carrying firearms being largely illiterate and serving as security guards. The regular constables, however, were literate and carried batons or short swords instead of guns. Police stations were under the command of either a head constable or sub-inspector. This system, introduced in all provinces, was unable to meet all problems. There were other police which functioned with various degrees of effectiveness, none of them very well. Railway police came into existence in 1861. They had, curiously, no responsibility for protecting railway property as such, but maintained order on trains and at stations, being authorized to carry out investigations where relevant crimes were involved. The problem with railway police was defining an effective area of jurisdiction. At first responsibility for railway security was placed in the hand of district police, but later responsibility was shifted to the provinces. Some experiments were made whereby police would function in connection with a railway or group of railways which operated in more than one province, and a nation-wide system was discussed. In the end the provincial system prevailed and provincial railway police were organized under an officer with the rank of superintendent. Criminals on the railways could be highly sophisticated, placing agents at arranged points along the line to receive stolen goods thrown out the windows of passing trains, while their associates gave warning of police presence on station platforms. It was not uncommon for them to slit the bags of sleeping travellers and, still undetected, sew them up after the desired goods had been removed.

The reforms of 1862 raised the question of the relations of the urban police commissioners in the presidency cities, Bombay, Madras and Calcutta, with the provincial inspector generals. In Bengal the Calcutta commissioner was completely independent of the inspector general. In Madras the commissioner, subordinate until 1887, became independent that year, and subordinate again in 1902. In Bombay no inspector general was appointed until 1874, after which he exercised no more than a nominal authority.

Darjeeling Police on parade.

No special arrangements were made for urban policing apart from the presidency cities.

Lord Curzon, whose administration as viceroy (1898-1905) would touch nearly every aspect of Indian government, was understandably concerned about police. Proceeding in the usual way he selected a commission to draw up a report. The commission, appointed in 1902, consisted of two Indian princes and five Europeans. Every aspect of policing came under consideration, but no total reorganization resulted. There would, however, be higher pay and more careful selection of personnel. Railway police were to be placed under a deputy inspector general of police in each province. An all-India Criminal Investigation Department (C.I.D.) was also organized which included a fingerprint bureau and co-ordinated police intelligence from all provinces. The most important innovation consisted of the organization of provincial training centres for newly appointed senior police officers, and smaller centres combining several districts for the training of constables. The course for senior officers lasted six months and included study of criminal law, the law of evidence, and practical work at the station level.

Relations between the collector and superintendent of police were discussed but no substantial changes made. Provincial inspector generals did not acquire cabinet rank in the provincial governments though it was made plain they should have regular consultations with the heads of those governments. The Indian princes on the commission raised the question of Indianization, but nothing was done until 1912 when competitive examinations for senior ranks were instituted simultaneously in England and India. A report in 1918 recommended the acceleration of Indianization, and a year later a quota of twenty-five per cent was set for Indians in higher ranks. This held until 1924, when it was decided that half of the new recruits should be Indian, a measure intended to increase the Indian quota to thirty per cent. If the desired quota could not be met by recruiting, it would be filled by promotion from the ranks. Although there were by the time of independence entire districts without a single European officer, the native Indian element in senior ranks stood at about thirty per cent in 1946.

As noted previously, in the frontier provinces necessity dictated raising special forces to control border tribes who lived at the subsistence level and for whom crime, especially raiding, was a way of life. These special forces, normally rather temporary, were constituted as part of tribal diplomacy whereby friendly native clan groupings, subsidized to act as police auxiliaries, proved effective as such. In 1913 on the Northwest Frontier a Frontier Constabulary of two thousand four hundred men was raised to deal with cross-border raids. This organization, which lived a Spartan existence against a background of permanent danger, gained an international reputation. A sister force on the Northeast Frontier had for its commander an explorer famous in his own time, J.F. Needham.

With the emergence of Indian nationalism in the twentieth century the police encountered a new challenge which often required military support. For a time an Irish Republican Army-style terrorism prevailed which involved the assassination of government officials followed by the murder of judges, prosecutors and witnesses involved in the conviction of terrorists. There was a full-scale revolt by the Moplahs, an Islamic sect, which involved attacks on the Hindu population. Yet by 1920 these activities were brought under control and never, when the total population of India is considered, reached Irish proportions. However, as independence appeared on the horizon tension increased between the Hindu and Muslim communities. This found expression in activities which bore some resemblance to those produced by Catholic-

Members of the Criminal Investigation Department, Poona.

Protestant antagonisms in Ireland, and even to those in Canada and the United States, particularly inasmuch as religious processions often marched through areas where their presence was calculated to give offence. In India, communal riots which disintegrated into looting and pogroms with great loss of life ensued. Indian mobs displayed remarkable ferocity but hardly more than the London mob in the Gordon Riots of 1780 or the participants in the New York Anti-Draft Riots of 1863. In many cases the Riot Act had to be read, and supported by a military presence.

The most remarkable development of the inter-war years was the emergence of the non-violent mass movement inspired by Mahatma Ghandi. Terrorism (politically-inspired violent crime), almost always the work of minorities, like "ordinary" non-political crime rarely attracted international sympathies, tending to remain on the back pages of newspapers. By contrast Ghandi, who in a sense followed in the steps of Daniel O'Connell, attracted much international sympathy. Although as in the case of O'Connell there was no acknowledgement, or visible understanding, between Ghandi and the police, they were unconscious allies. Ghandi, who possessed considerable political wisdom, must have realized that the propaganda successes he achieved pre-supposed the existence of a disciplined police which acted within the law.

Nothing more clearly demonstrated the need for effective police than the disaster at Amritsar, commonly known as the Amritsar Massacre. In 1919 when Ghandi proclaimed a campaign of civil disobedience, riots in the aforementioned city went beyond non-violent protest. For reasons unexplained, the armed police reserve of twenty-five men remained in the *kotwali* and little use was made of the hundred unarmed constables also locally available to the authorities in Amritsar. The hostile and aggressive mob, gathered in an enclosed square, has often been described as unarmed but in reality its members brandished *lathi* (iron-tipped bamboo spears). The military were called out and on the order of General Reginald Dyer his Gurkha troops repeatedly fired on the crowd, killing three hundred and seventy-nine and leaving about twelve-hundred wounded.

Ghandi called off the campaign but resumed activities the following year. The new effort involved a boycott of police which gained popular support but when it degenerated into violence it was also called off. Yet another attempt met cancellation in 1922 after a mob killed twenty-two police. Ghandi made his point: that he would under no provocation resort to physical force. Although he exercised an imperfect control of his followers, he impressed world opinion by his repeated repudiation of violence which could be associated with his name. After spending two years in jail he resumed activity in 1930 and led a two hundred and forty mile salt march, designed to defy the salt supply monopoly of the government. From the police point of view this involved masses in political action who indulged in systematic harassment of law officers. On the other hand it denied public attention to those prepared to use terrorism and other forms of violence. Altogether sixty thousand were at one time or another arrested during the salt march and several hundred injured by police, but there was no second Amritsar. Ghandi did not win immediate independence. As the public lost interest in political action until World War II, Ghandi's later non-violence campaign collapsed. Indeed, he was arrested and the Congress party declared illegal.

Except during the salt march, Ghandi exercised a limited control over his followers. As noted, they frequently ignored his instructions to refrain from attacks on the police. Yet the types of demonstrations he authorized, even those that contrary to his orders used violence against the police, could have been suppressed with a few volleys. The police, by accepting verbal abuse and physical punishment while keeping their reaction in most cases under control, left Ghandi in the centre of the stage, even when he was under arrest. Ghandi was prepared to take over the state created by the British, and reshape it to suit his ideas, but not to leave security at the mercy of mob violence.

In the late eighteenth and early nineteenth centuries the British Empire by degrees moved into the vacuum left by the collapse of the Moghul one. In the process it was unable to revive the traditional Indian police institutions. Until 1861-1862 the British groped for a policy, leaning increasingly on military-style police. From that time on, using the Irish model, they created an imperfect but competent civil police which with many modifications has survived independence.

CHAPTER VII

POLICE IN AUSTRALIA

USTRALIA STARTED AS A PENAL colony at a time when Britain was beginning to accept the need for bureaucratic government. Thus the Australians were not left to themselves, like the early settlers in America, to make the best they could of mediaeval English institutions. Apart from this, Australian police institutions matured before Confederation of the states in 1900. Consequently the country did not develop a federal police in the manner of Canada. Australian police evolved separately in each of the colonies, which became states.

The penal colony began in 1788 when Captain Arthur Philips of the Royal Navy arrived in what was known as Botany Bay, with eleven ships carrying seven hundred and seventeen convicts, of whom five hundred and twenty were men. Philips, who held the official power of a prison warden, unlike most colonial governors had no appointed council to assist or restrain him. He was something of a secular idealist, honest, severe, and determined to do his best. Under the title of captain general of New South Wales he exercised power there until 1792. Philips' first problem arose when the Royal Marines refused to do police duties. With supplies short, the captain general found it necessary to appoint twelve of the more reliable convicts as a night watch, who thereby became the first police in Australia. In the course of their duties the watchmen apprehended six marines breaking into the depleted stores. These Philips arrested and, after an investigation, hanged in spite of the protests of their officers.

The watch continued in their duties and appear to have evolved into constables. Military officers served as magistrates and a system developed whereby constables were in theory elected, but in practice appointed from among freed or trustworthy convicts. They were clothed, housed and fed by the government, and paid in rum which became the only effective currency in the settlement. The marines were replaced as guards with the arrival of the second fleet in 1790. Aboard was the New South Wales Corps, a unit recruited in Britain for service in the colony. Its commander, Major Francis Grose, took over from Philips in 1792.

Before long the colony progressed to the point where convict labour could be farmed out to free settlers, mostly officers and former officers, whose problem was to provide the convicts with an incentive to work. Rum proved the answer, and as the officers were in a position to acquire rum in large quantities, they settled in as relatively prosperous farmers with a largely convict labour supply. After Grose left the settlement in 1794, however, matters soon got out of hand. There were at the same time fears that the Irish political exiles in the colony would, after the outbreak of war with France, attempt some kind of a rebellion. This led to the creation of an "armed association" which did act to put down a feeble attempt at revolt in 1804.

The introduction of sheep gave the colony a link with the international market, and in so doing increased the wealth and power of the New South Wales Corps whose members had increasingly become entrepreneurs and begun to consider themselves as constituting a local aristocracy. Captain William Bligh, best known for his command of the mutinous H.M.S. *Bounty*, sought to bring the officers and former officers under control, and taking the bull by the horns, he arrested on contrived evidence Captain John MacArthur who, among other things, first brought sheep to New South Wales. This brought on a full-scale rebellion, during which Bligh found himself deposed and placed under house arrest. The mutineers appealed to London for vindication, meanwhile remaining in power for two years until Colonel Lachlan Macquarrie arrived as governor in 1809. Bligh returned to England, and the

New South Wales Corps was replaced by Macquarrie's regiment, the 104th.

Macquarrie saw the penal colony as a means of providing a second chance in life to convicts. To this end he was prepared to appoint former convicts as jurymen and even justices of the peace, which put him at odds with the growing community of free settlers. In police arrangements Macquarrie appointed a small military patrol for Sydney, dividing the town into five districts with six constables to each under the overall authority of a head constable, and made a beginning in keeping crime statistics. Constables carried a cutlass, and the usual rattle which in the eighteenth and nineteenth centuries served the same purposes a whistle did subsequently. The surgeon, D'Arcy Wentworth, eventually was given the title of superintendent of police. Protests by free settlers against Macquarrie's efforts to employ former convicts in administration led to the appointment of a one-man commission in the person of John T. Bigge, a London barrister. In his report Bigge stated that the future of Australia belonged to free settlers, but convict labour remained useful to open up the country. Macquarrie's ideal was rejected and Sir Thomas Brisbane replaced him in 1821, being assisted after 1823 by an appointed council. Bigge's report recommended that all police in the colony should be placed under a single official. As a result of this Captain F. N. Rossi was given the title of superintendent of all New South Wales police. Yet his actual authority never extended much beyond Sydney, and he remained unable to do much to meet what was becoming the chief police problem of Australia, bush ranging.

Bush rangers were generally either escaped convicts or those, having served their term, who moved into the interior to prey upon aboriginals and isolated settlers. With the development of roads along which valuables moved, they also became highwaymen, soon passing into folklore as popular heroes who defied authority. As they could not be dealt with by sedentary police, a tentative effort followed on the governor's initiative in 1825 to organize a highway patrol. Recruited from the military and made up initially of two officers and thirteen troopers uniformed and armed as light cavalry, this force would grow and become the prototype for Australian rural police. However, difficulties proved such that for several years their efforts to reduce criminal activity met with indifferent success, and the council in 1830 thought it necessary to pass the Bush Ranger Act. This legislation authorized the police to arrest suspicious persons without warrant and detain them until they could give a satisfactory account of themselves. Meanwhile trial by jury was introduced for criminal cases, former convicts being permitted with some exceptions to serve as jurors. For their part, the mounted police reached a strength of one hundred and sixty by 1840, the year the practice of transporting of convicts to New South Wales terminated. At that time the force was divided into three highway patrol units, each commanded by a captain with Captain John McLerie at headquarters acting as paymaster and senior man.

A mounted trooper in Australia.

In Sydney, Rossi faced such a personnel turnover in his underpaid and under-disciplined force that his successor, H.C. Wilson, recommended recruiting in Britain. This policy, when put into effect, brought in some respects a better class of recruit to Sydney, but too many of them were men getting on in years who had difficulty in coming to terms with the rough and tumble of colonial society. Matters became further complicated in 1834 when the cost of police was transferred from the imperial to the local budget. Wilson attempted to make the London Metropolitan Police his model, amongst other things introducing uniforms. Despite long hours and meagre pay, the Sydney force grew from seventy-six in 1832 to a hundred and eighty-one in 1838. A New Year's riot in 1850 led to an investigation and a report which echoed the complaints of every police superintendent   low pay and the poor quality of recruits. In an effort to improve matters Captain John McLerie of the mounted police was appointed to the newly-created office of inspector general of New South Wales police, which post he held until 1874.

By mid-century responsible government was already a fact in Canada, and the British parliament had passed the Australian Government Act which gave Australian colonies the power to write their own constitutions subject to British approval. The island of Tasmania, first settled in 1803, became an independent jurisdiction in 1825, Western Australia in 1829, South Australia in 1841, Victoria ten years later and Queensland in 1859. The advent of Victoria as a separate political entity was contemporary with the discovery of gold, which increased the population from seventy-seven thousand in 1851 to three hundred and thirty-three thousand in 1855. This resulted in shantytown, boom or bust conditions similar to those found in California in 1849 and in the Yukon in 1898. While still under the jurisdiction of Sydney, Victoria had organized four police forces: a town foot constabulary; a mounted force; a native corps; and a water police. For a time border police also existed, but were disbanded in 1840. None of these forces were large. The native police, who were mounted, numbered forty-four in 1844, the mounted police mustering only twenty-nine. Although wages were doubled, reaching six shillings a day, this proved insufficient against the temptations of instant wealth in the goldfields. Hard-pressed, the Victoria legislature authorized the recruiting of eight hundred men in Britain. Of these some fifty arrived in 1853 under the command of Inspector Samuel Freeman. Henceforth the Victoria police, following in the footsteps of New South Wales but with much greater success, became a model for other colonies.

In the goldfields the burden of law enforcement fell on the native mounted police who were ridiculed as "Joes." As a source of

An Australian trooper on patrol.

revenue the government decided that miners (diggers, as they became almost universally known in Australia) must purchase a licence, thus imposing on the police the unpopular task of arresting unlicenced searchers for fortune. The fee (thirty shillings a month) was considered high and police methods of collecting it high-handed. For example, when prisoners were in transit to captivity, in the absence of a local jail they were chained to trees. The diggers did what they could to frustrate police efforts, with constant agitation accompanied by threats of revolt. On the whole the British element insisted on lawful protest, but the German and Irish miners talked openly of armed insurrection. The vacillating policy of Lieutenant Governor Joseph La Trobe did not much improve relations between miners and police, while a rising became a certainty with the arrival of his stiff-necked naval officer successor, Sir Charles Hotham.

Nothing remained but the required incident to set off a full-scale revolt. This occurred with the acquittal of an obviously guilty innkeeper charged with the murder of a drunken miner. At the outset matters had the character of vigilantism as a mob took justice into their own hands and destroyed the offending innkeeper's tavern. The man's acquittal was subsequently reversed by the higher courts, but the ringleaders of the riot were prosecuted. There followed scenes which might well have taken place in America if the United States authorities had stood up to vigilantism. The miners demanded release of the accused, and when the government made no concessions they turned to an eloquent leader in Peter Lalor, who would later turn to more conventional politics. A mass burning of licences followed as an act of defiance and a Southern Cross flag was raised while the miners constructed a fortified camp which became known as the Eureka Stockade. When the prospect of real violence approached, however, most of those of British background withdrew. They shared the grievances of fellow diggers with respect to the government licencing policy, but participation in violence against crown forces which could be construed as treason was another matter. Their departure left Lalor with a force of about a hundred and fifty out of an original two thousand. On the morning of the 2nd of December 1854 a mixed body of police and, mostly, military moved in on the Eureka Stockade. The two hundred and seventy-six men attacking the miners' defensive position included twenty mounted and twenty-four foot police; and in the ensuing battle they killed thirty of their opponents while taking one hundred and fourteen prisoners. Of these, thirteen later faced trial for treason, all being acquitted. Lalor evaded capture.

While the revolt at the Eureka Stockade could be justified by miners' grievances against government policies which were insensitive if not provocative, no such redeeming feature marked the outbreak at Lambing Flats, New South Wales, in 1861. The slogans and talk of miners' rights sounded much the same, and the Southern Cross flag flew again. Yet there resemblances ended. This time the complaint was not digging licences, but the presence of Chinese on the fringe of the miners' encampment. Xenophobia is at least as strong among frontiersmen as is resentment of authority. The five thousand or so miners in Lambing Flats were easily convinced that the Chinese encamped near them at Tipperary Gully must be driven out. When the newly organized Miners' Protection League passed a resolution to that effect the police, anticipating no immediate trouble, took no preventative measures. Over a thousand diggers, many armed, struck without warning, destroying huts and tents as well as appropriating the earnings and goods of the Chinese. Police reaction was immediate, as the sergeant in charge of the local post arrested the leaders of the raid and called for reinforcements. The miners meanwhile gathered in a crowd of several thousand, demanding release of the prisoners. The police, commanded by Captain Henry Zouch and Gold Commissioner J.T. Griffin, had by now been reinforced, though still numbering something less than a hundred men. Brief negotiations with the miners followed, during which the mob's leaders were permitted to interview the prisoners. When this merely resulted in further threats, the reading of the Riot Act followed and the police twice charged and twice dispersed the crowd, killing eight miners.

While the diggers prepared to launch a general attack on his post the next day, Zouch judiciously slipped away with his now desperately beleaguered garrison together with the prisoners. There ensued destruction of the police station and other government property, together with the seizure of arms and ammunition from local stores, as the more peaceful-minded of the area's inhabitants fled to the hills. However for all that there was no fight, for upon arrival of a large if improvised government contingent including some naval personnel besides the usual troops and police, resistance collapsed.

Yet the Lambing Flats incident highlighted the limitations of existing police arrangements, particularly the prevalence of separate jurisdictions which made cooperation difficult. A solution appeared in the Police Act of 1862 which adopted the system of the Irish (after 1867, Royal Irish) Constabulary, with Inspector General McLerie remaining in command. While New South Wales and Victoria reorganized their police structure, the other colonies, faced with similar difficulties, found similar answers.

Tasmania, however, represented in a sense a special case, as it was founded as the place where the hard cases were sent. Very early police magistrates were given authority to deal with minor crime, a superintendent of police being appointed in 1815. Constables were to be drawn from free men when possible, but failing that from the better class of convicts. In the capital, Hobart, a night patrol was set up, enforcing a curfew which began at dusk. Records were kept of all inhabitants, the island being divided into police districts, each under a police magistrate who commanded a force of constables and a detachment of more mobile field police. The entire organization answered to a chief police magistrate residing in Hobart.

After 1841 Tasmanian convicts were no longer assigned to specific employers, but enjoyed a probationary status. Two years later the chief magistrate became probation officer, and by 1845 the police in the manner of the Irish Constabulary collected social and economic statistics, providing at the same time a useful link between government and people. The coming of responsible government to Tasmania in 1856 saw police districts reorganized to conform to electoral districts, with provision made for municipalities controlling and financing their own forces. Finally in 1898 all police were centralized under the command of a commissioner responsible to the executive. Yet the administrative development of Tasmanian law enforcement does not tell the whole story. The police and military proved unable or insufficiently concerned to prevent the extermination of the island's aboriginals, who suffered the depredations of escaped convicts and similar vicious elements. Like the Beothuks of Newfoundland, they ceased to exist as a people.

South Australia, west of Victoria, never an area of convict settlement, started as a social experiment inspired by the English visionary Edward Gibbon Wakefield. The idea was to populate the colony with a more prosperous type of settler by keeping the price of land high. In practice it proved a formula for disorder which prevailed until George Grey became governor in 1841. Small bodies of police were formed in the early years before the arrival of Major S. O'Halloran who took command in 1840. O'Halloran met some success in coping with convict immigrants from the other colonies and the hostile aboriginals who raided frontier settlements; and on departing from office in 1843 he left in place a reasonably competent force, similar to those in Victoria and New South Wales. The low pay of three shillings, six pence a day of the early years improved with the addition of new responsibilities, rising to six shillings by the end of the century. In comparison, the Canadian North West Mounted Police received at the same time only seventy-five cents.

Fanny Bay Jail, Darwin.

The great challenge to the South Australia police came in 1863 when the colony assigned them the administration of the interior and northern regions of the continent. At first largely involved in exploration and laying telegraph lines, it also became for them a matter of desert patrol in which horses could not survive the climate for long and bullocks, who fared better, could cover only ten miles a day. In 1860 the Victoria police had imported camels from India to use in exploration work as the animals could travel up to eighty-four miles in eighteen hours, and go for prover-bially long periods without water. They were obviously suited to police work in desert terrain, being adopted for regular service by the South Australia police in 1866. Curiously, efforts to employ camels in the United States were the subject of a pamphlet written before the Civil War by Jefferson Davis, subsequently president of the Confederate States of America, while he was still an officer in the U.S. army. They were tried for a time in the south west, but not used extensively because they did not breed in America. In the more congenial climate of Australia camels bred freely, and they became a permanent feature of life in the interior.

Western Australia made a start at a police force as early as 1829, but remained a backwater until the introduction of convict labour in 1850. This stimulated development yet at the same time brought a crime wave as convicts took to the bush where they as usual abused the natives and provoked reprisals directed against settlements. Aboriginals who previously merely killed or stole cattle now began to attack settlers. A small military guard had been pro-vided in 1848 and constables were added in various districts in 1850, creating a force numbering eighty-seven, partly European and partly aboriginal, partly convict and partly free. Among them served eleven mounted aboriginal troopers and twenty convict mounted police. These men, who collectively constituted what was known as the Enrolled Force, worked under a superintendent of police, their task being surveillance of convict gangs of road work-ers who were in turn under the direct control of a warden. This involved the pursuit of escaped convicts and general patrol of the extensive territory of the colony (975,920 square miles). Reorganization came in 1861 with Superintendent A. Hogan, with the division of the colony into police districts, each under a superintendent, the senior officer soon being designated a commissioner, supported by inspectors, sub-inspectors, sergeants, detectives, corporals and constables. There was thus an R.I.C.-style force in being in Western Australia when convict labour ended in 1868.

The most demanding task of the force involved patrol of the northern region of Western Australia with its scarcity of water. In this sparsely populated area crime could not be concealed for long, and criminals left trails. Pursuit was usually a matter of tracking with the aid of aboriginal auxiliaries. As in other colonies wages were high, constables receiving from six shillings and six pence to nine shillings a day. By the turn of the century promotion was from the ranks, including promotion to the highest rank, that of commissioner.

In 1911 the Northern Territories were transferred from the jurisdiction of South Australia to the federal government. At that time there were no more than thirty or so police employed in the territories, individual troopers before the coming of the automobile travelling up to four thousand miles a year on horseback. Also in the north, sub-tropical Queensland, which became a separate jurisdiction in 1859, was in every sense a special case. Until 1842 the military conducted all police work. In that year a chief constable and five constables were appointed as a gesture, but not until 1848 with the formation of the Native Mounted Force did police in Queensland become significantly effective. Yet even this body was disbanded after a few years, then reconstituted in 1852 after the discovery of gold. Tribal rivalries were such that each detachment had to be recruited from the same group, there being a danger that the police if not restrained by their officers would use weapons to kill members of rival tribes. By 1864 the police were about equally divided with a hundred and fifty Europeans and a hundred and thirty-seven native personnel. Toward the end of the century the native component was phased out, with the last troopers kept on as trackers. Stability in the force was provided by the long service of D.T. Seymour, who commanded for thirty years. Links with the Royal Irish Constabulary were provided by the appointment as commissioner of Major W.G. Cahill, who had served in the R.I.C. Cahill served twelve years, including during the early years of World War I. By that time the force numbered over a thousand in a population of less than seven hundred thousand. Pay was high as in the other colonies, or states as they were called after Confederation in 1900. Yet glaring contrasts existed, European constables receiving £108 to £130 a year, but native trackers only about £18.

The great achievement of the police in most colonies was the suppression of the bush rangers, who provided something of an Australian counterpart to the outlaws of the American wild west. On the whole the bush rangers deserved their place in folk-lore. They could be ruthless but were tough and resourceful criminals whose exploits would appeal to a population with a large element historically disposed to resent authority in any form. The first bush rangers were convicts or ex-convicts who took full advantage of an under-policed society. They were always formidable but in the aftermath of the various goldrushes a special problem arose with large numbers of unemployed former prospectors. As the extraction of gold was taken over by large companies, attacks on gold shipments were an obvious temptation, and one likely to win a certain amount of popular sympathy. Very often bush rangers made conscious efforts to create their own myths. Outstanding among these was Francis Gardiner, who wrote letters to the press ridiculing the police whom he out-manoeuvred. Gardiner was eventually captured and sentenced to thirty-two years in prison, but his popularity was such that he was released after serving only a third of his term and sent out of the country. He then moved to San Francisco and spent the rest of his days, so far as is known, as an honest man.

Most spectacular were the Kelly gang, a criminal family, who commenced serious crime with the murder of troopers sent to arrest them. In February 1877 Ned Kelly, in the course of a bank robbery, captured the local police and took over the town of Jerilderie in New South Wales, and while doing so compelled the school master to write a note giving the children a day's holiday. The Kellys came to a dramatic end in June 1880 when they seized the station master's house at Glenrowan, tore up the tracks to wreck the expected pursuit, and held the local population prisoners in the station. The police, being warned, avoided the planned train wreck, and the Kellys were forced to stand siege. They made no attempt at hostage-taking, and in a display of a rough sort of chivalry permitted the release of their prisoners. In the ensuing gunfight Ned Kelly attacked the police in an improvised suit of armour, which proved bullet-proof. Kelly exchanged fire with the police for twenty minutes until brought down by a shot in the leg. The fight ended with the station set on fire, and its inmates killed. Ned Kelly was captured, recovered from his wound, and duly tried and executed.

In spite of the legends that surround them, and their spectacular exploits, the bush rangers could not withstand the constant pressure of the trooper police. On the whole, despite some parallels, there was nothing like the American wild west in Australia. The country's police were by the end of the century the best trained and, apart from those in the United States, the best paid in the world. The urban police followed as far as they could the London model, but the rural mounted police, which included many ex-R.I.C. members in their ranks, was of R.I.C. inspiration. Age limits were from twenty-one to twenty-nine, recruits having to be physically fit, literate and of good character. Successful applicants trained in a depot as vacancies occurred. Probationary constables first trained as cavalrymen, then after a probationary period of up to twelve months received instruction in law and the various duties which involved collecting agricultural statistics and other information.

Once in the field the constable was often the only regular link between outlying settlements and the state. Among the powers given a constable was the authority to perform marriages, as often no clergyman or justice of the peace lived within miles of isolated settlements or homesteads. In the twentieth century much of this would change with the coming of motor transport and airplanes. Yet the Australian trooper police for a period covering several generations indeed represented for many settlers in the interior the only effective link with civilization.

CHAPTER VIII

SOUTH AFRICAN POLICE

THE DUTCH WERE THE FIRST Europeans to colonize South Africa, just as they were the first to settle what is now New York. Jan Van Riebeck arrived at the Cape of Good Hope in 1652, some thirty-two years after his countrymen established a post on Manhattan Island. Riebeck at once proclaimed martial law, assigning police work to the military. Within a year a *skout* or chief constable was appointed, assisted by Caffres from the East Indies banished to the Cape Colony, thus anticipating the Australian employment of convict police by approximately a century and a half. By 1689 a fiscal or treasury official held control, on Dutch East India Company authority exercising both judicial and police power. The latter included the right to conscript former soldiers for policing and other duties. A ten man night watch commanded by a sergeant and provided with rattles which could raise "hue and cry" in case of serious disturbances served for what became Cape Town. In rural areas the chief official was the field cornet, a semi-military version of the justice of the peace. As these officers could hardly provide adequate services for widely scattered settlements, there was also sometimes recourse to police *rerits*, bounty-hunting private agents much like the London thief-takers though operating in a very different milieu.

The British, who began their occupation in 1795, left existing arrangements in force as they ruled in the name of the house of Orange which had been driven into exile when the armies of the

French Revolution advanced into Holland. In spite of formal British annexation of the Cape Colony in 1814, Dutch law and language prevailed until 1822. Not before 1828 did the justice of the peace replace the Dutch magistrates or *landrosts*. After that the process of institutional Anglicization accompanied by the arrival of British immigrants increased cultural tensions which led to the Great Trek north in the mid-1830s. The Dutch farmers (numbers of them actually of Huguenot and German Protestant background also) or Boers in the outlying settlements, the *voor trekkers*, moved into the interior where they established two loosely organized independent republics. Since they constituted a culturally rather homogeneous, very piously Protestant group, they manifested comparatively little internal crime, but police arrangements were required to protect livestock from the raids of natives. The solution lay in the organization of the commando, an informal body of armed and mounted farmers under a field cornet.

In the Transvaal, the stronger of the two republics, the discovery of diamonds and gold stimulated urbanization. With it came the creation of a *sergeanten van polite* or police force, while burghers were reminded of their duty to apprehend vagabonds and vagrants and turn them over to field cornets. At the same time a border police was organized to deal with the infiltration and raids of Zulu tribesmen. The other Boer republic, the Orange Free State, had a similar history, municipal police being established in most towns by 1873, border police having been founded 11 years earlier. As in the American west, an armed and mounted population lived in an atmosphere of permanent insecurity. Under these conditions self-policing was a possible, if not the most effective, means of providing protection.

Most of South Africa was under British control, with two major divisions, Natal and the Cape Colony, which each developed its own police institutions. Natal, taken by the British in 1843 to prevent the trek Boers from acquiring an outlet to the sea, was placed under the Cape Colony in 1844 and became an independent jurisdiction in 1856. The Cape, the more urban of the two colonies, made efforts to introduce the London Metropolitan Police system in 1840, establishing the Cape Constabulary, after 1882 called the Cape Police. With the growth of population local forces were appointed in larger towns, complete with a plain clothes detective force. The countryside, as in the Boer republics, remained largely self-policing, as serious trouble was confined to the border areas. Constant cross-border native raids for cattle stealing resulted in occasional punitive expeditions. These demanded a special type of police trained and equipped for military service.

Miscellaneous organizations provided frontier defence. There existed an auxiliary force recruited from among the Hottentots, the original inhabitants of the Cape area, who proved to be too much in awe of the Kaffirs, then moving into the Cape, to be effective. There were also under-disciplined Cape Town levies, drawn from all races, and several better-disciplined volunteer forces raised by private individuals; but the main burden of frontier defence fell on the Cape Mounted Rifles. As early as 1797 a corps drawn from the Hottentot tribe was placed under a lieutenant of the 98th Foot. By 1800 this body was formed into a regiment under a lieutenant colonel. When the colony returned temporarily to Dutch control in 1802, this corps remained in being. In 1806 when the area again became British, the regiment came under the command of Major John Graham, who by 1808 had expanded the force to eight hundred. By 1812 the entire regiment served on the eastern frontier with headquarters at Grahamstown. In their patrol work on the frontier the men of the Cape Mounted Rifles returned stolen cattle, also being encouraged to when possible bring in prisoners, for which rewards were paid. Between 1822 and 1840 the force, expanded over the years to include four troops of cavalry and four of infantry, recovered over six thousand head of cattle and three hundred or so horses.

A sergeant of the Native Police.

The Cape Mounted Rifles at the peak of their efficiency numbered eight hundred strong, two-thirds being natives. They were armed with smooth-bore double-barrelled carbines (in effect, shotguns) which could be easily loaded on horseback. Like the North West Mounted Police in Canada, they trained to serve on both horseback and foot. Rather than the scarlet tunics of the Canadian Mounties, however, they wore dark green uniforms similar to those of British rifle regiments, their mounts being carefully chosen and sold to the men for £25. The old Cape Mounted Rifles were disbanded in 1857, then reconstituted as the Frontier Armed and Mounted Police, reverting to their original name, the Cape Mounted Rifles, in 1878. During the Frontier Police period numbers of men were enlisted in Britain, such volunteers being provided with passage in difficult steerage class conditions where they often found themselves obliged to fight for their food. Recruits had to buy their own horses, often at inflated prices. Morale was low and desertion common amongst those recruited both in Britain and locally, except in an artillery battery with a more selective choice of personnel. Much of the trouble lay in the attempt to impose regular army cavalry-style discipline on what originated as a rough and ready frontier corps. When the Frontier Armed and Mounted Police again assumed the name the Cape Mounted Rifles, they were re-organized in two wings, each under the command of a lieutenant colonel under the over-all supervision of a general officer. The Cape Mounted Rifles remained a frontier, paramilitary police, and are not to be confused with the Cape Mounted Police who were organized for internal rural patrol in 1904.

The Cape achieved responsible government in 1872 but it did not come to the sister colony of Natal until 1893. Consequently the problem of policing remained in that colony for several decades longer the responsibility of the colonial office. Natal emerged amid a series of Zulu Wars in which sedentary police played only a small role. By 1874 the European population numbered seventeen thousand, together with thirty thousand Indians and about five hundred thousand blacks. The colony was governed by an appointed council though, while resident magistrates dealt with the European and Indian populations, in the tribal areas real authority rested with the chieftains and the government exercised virtually no control over tribal politics. Nothing prevented an ambitious and able leader from seizing power, organizing his people for war, and building up a tribal federation by conquering or intimidating his neighbours. In Natal's early years there existed no alternative to military law enforcement, provided by British regulars and local volunteers. The occasion for the formation of what became the Natal Mounted Police was a rebellion led by the Hlubi chieftain Langalibalele in 1873.

The Natal Mounted Police were the creation of Major J.G. Dartnell, a retired veteran of the Crimea and the Indian Mutiny as well as many small colonial campaigns, then serving as a commander of volunteers. Dartnell saw that the obvious model for his force was the Cape Mounted Rifles, yet they were a frontier corps with limited responsibilities, whereas the Natal force would have to patrol an entire province including tribal areas requiring not only general policing but the prevention of inter-tribal warfare. Dartnell received authorization to recruit fifty Europeans at five shillings, six pence a day, out of which as in the Cape Mounted Rifles three shillings went to provide rations for themselves and their horses. Moreover, the men had to purchase their own mounts. Native troopers received only fifteen shillings a month, though with rations and uniforms provided. Native corporals earned seventeen shillings and sergeants twenty-two per month. Skilled labour could command better pay; hence Dartnell experienced trouble keeping men in the force. As far as Europeans were concerned, he recommended following the example of the Cape Mounted Rifles by recruiting in Britain.

Adjutant of the Natal Police.

While the original intention was to follow the Mounted Rifles' model of two native troopers to each European, after some difficulties with government bureaucracy Dartnell reversed the ratio of Europeans to natives in his force, and found suitable uniforms, horses and weapons. In 1875 he initiated full-scale policing of tribal areas, a move which gave more effective authority to isolated magistrates previously frequently limited to mere mediation between contending tribal chieftains. Although the troopers in the early days faced the usual abuse from the press, they soon proved their usefulness. When the Zulu threat induced the Transvaal to accept British annexation in 1877, the Natal Mounted Police constituted the only British force present for an uneasy week until the regular army arrived. They fought as soldiers in the Zulu War of the late 1870s, a detachment being wiped out in the British debacle at Isandhlwana in January 1879. However, a member of the force, fighting beside the regular South Wales Borderers very shortly thereafter, won one of the record number of Victoria Crosses awarded for a single engagement during the successful defence of Rorke's Drift against seemingly impossible odds. Later, Natal Mounted Police played an instrumental role in capturing the Zulu King Cetawayo. They also escorted the former Empress of France when she visited the site of the death of her son, killed in action while serving against the Zulus with the British.

Full military service was demanded during the first Boer War of Independence in 1881, and again during the Boer War of 1899-1902. The Natal Mounted Police proved effective in policing whites also, yet tribal-related responsibilities remained. In this connection they were for over a generation supported by the Zululand Mounted Police recruited by Inspector G. Mansel to guard the British residents in Zululand. The latter force were first a body of sixty known as the Carbineers, but increased to two hundred and fifty under the Zululand name in 1888. The Zululand Mounted Police, fighting side-by-side with British regulars, very early gave a good account of themselves, inflicting heavy casualties on native warriors who often far out-numbered them. During the Boer War they were incorporated into the Natal Mounted Police, being disbanded in 1904 and temporarily reconstituted during a rebellion in 1906, after which they finally ceased to exist.

In 1894 the Natal Mounted Police took over the Water Police, whose duties involved boarding ships and dealing with immigrants as well as regulating tariffs on the waterfront. This mixed force of about a hundred was an integral part of the police, frequently commanded

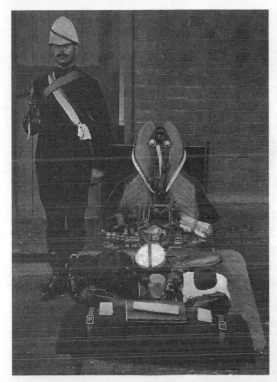

The uniform and kit of the Natal Mounted Police in the late nineteenth century.

The Water Police.

by officers who had served in the interior. The same year, 1894, the Natal Mounted Police absorbed the Railway Police, which at the time consisted of two Europeans and thirty coloured constables. This unit thereafter expanded to nearly one hundred, but its activities still did not go much beyond crime detection in cases involving railways.

The Boer War, when it came, was by some optimistic British circles expected to be short. After the inevitable imperial victory, it was believed the main immediate challenge would be the avoidance of the kind of social tensions and disintegration which marked the Reconstruction period after the American Civil War. Adequate and impartial policing appeared to be the answer, and the man selected to bring into being the necessary force was Major General Robert Baden-Powell, the future organizer of the Boy Scouts. He already enjoyed the status of a war hero for his gallant and imaginative defence of the town of Kimberley. By the same token, unlike many professional soldiers he demonstrated a flair for improvisation and put great reliance on the use of talent in the rank and file. Baden-Powell's mandate as of October 1900 was to raise a force of ten thousand to be ready by mid-1901, the assumption being that by then the war would be over and an abundance of military stores, horses and recruits available. This assumption proved wrong, as the conflict was to last another two years. Baden-Powell hence faced the challenge of raising suitable personnel, horses and equipment where he could; and, with the war continuing, his men would for a time be expected to conduct military operations.

He proved equal to the task, and had on his side the fact that he was a war hero. To recruit officers, he went to a camp at Stellenbasch, which he described as a military purgatory for those who had made serious mistakes. Yet these men's former lapses notwithstanding, they presented him with a nucleus of trained leadership material while ultimately Baden-Powell received twelve thousand applications to fill three hundred officer vacancies. He at the same time recruited six hundred loyal Cape Colony Boers, and some two thousand Zulus. Most of the rest of the personnel of all ranks came from all over the empire, candidates being required to pass a medical examination as well as riding and shooting tests at home before being sent out. Finger prints were taken at each test and signed by the examiner, thus ensuring that those recruited abroad would be the same individuals who turned up for service. Baden-Powell established his post at a former dynamite factory between Johannesburg and Pretoria, and began training recruits as they arrived. He designed a special khaki uniform with a view to comfort and efficiency in the field; and this, together with its stetson hat, later provided the model for the original Boy Scout uniform.

In matter of training Baden-Powell placed emphasis on the ability to operate in small self-reliant groups and to think independently. The force, designated the South African Constabulary (the S.A.C.), was organized in four divisions, three under regular British senior officers and one under Colonel Sam Steele of the Canadian Royal North West Mounted Police. A New Zealander headed the veterinary department, while nurses in the medical unit wore special uniforms, also designed by Baden-Powell, which included the stetson hat. Pay was $1.25 a day, but all found. The men were provided with no pension though it was hoped that members of the force would in due course accept land grants and, for a retainer of £12, form a police reserve. Horses represented a particular problem as the army was buying all the local stock. Baden-Powell met this difficulty by importing mounts from Australia, though of a size on average smaller than the army standard. As these imported horses could not bear the strain of working at altitudes of four to five thousand feet, they were first acclimatised at a special farm acquired for the purpose. Once trained, the constabulary units were sent to the army for active service, and soon became experts in anti-guerrilla warfare. By June of 1901 Baden-Powell had a force of eight thousand men in the field.

Before the war's end the men of the S.A.C. had won three Victoria Crosses and several Distinguished Service Orders, but their organizer and commander, feeling this recognition to be insufficient, instituted a special badge for gallantry. However, only with the return of peace in 1902 did real policing begin, the over-all objective of the constabulary being to win the confidence of their former enemies. The men, accordingly, were encouraged not only to learn the Boer language, Afrikaans, but to improve their fluency by speaking it among themselves. As an abundance of volunteers existed, it proved the more possible to dismiss unsatisfactory troopers. Although the award of direct commissions was the practice at the beginning, promotion from the ranks was possible and practical as among his recruits were some two thousand public school boys. Candidates for commissions had to pass several tests and to have served satisfactorily in four different squadrons.

By the time peace was declared on the 24th of May 1902 the S.A.C. stood at ten thousand five hundred men, the largest mounted police force in the world. Their first task was to prepare a register of the Transvaal and Orange Free State population, derived from documents in the government archives of the former republics. Things did not, however, in all cases run as smoothly as this exercise in book-keeping. At the end of hostilities the Boer population was disarmed but the native Kaffirs, who had for the most part supported the British in the late conflict, still kept their weapons. Sam Steele protested against this policy, and insisted upon also disarming the Kaffirs who were harassing the now vulnerable Boer farmers. He did not obtain authorization for this until September 1902, but in the interim restrained the Kaffirs by the employment of Zulu police constables, insisting that there be at least one with every detachment. When the disarming was finally carried out, the Kaffirs received monetary compensation for arms taken up, of which there were ten thousand two hundred and forty in Steele's district. One unexpected consequence of this policy of disarmament was a proliferation of wildlife, particularly baboons, who destroyed crops and drove women and children indoors. It accordingly fell to the S.A.C. to reduce the wildlife to manageable proportions, and men who had been pursuing Boer commandos for a time found themselves hunting another order of creature.

The process of winning over the population was enhanced by offering mail and medical services never before provided. More important still was modern veterinary help given in detecting cattle diseases and quarantining infected stock. Steele experienced particular trouble in his efforts to prevent the movement of diseased cattle from Portuguese Africa into the Transvaal. Civilian officials resisted the efforts of his border patrols to halt the movement of infected livestock across the frontier on the grounds that they must honour entrance permits. At the same time game department personnel protested against the presence of police in game reserves.

One of the greatest difficulties arose from the fact that S.A.C. officers possessed no judicial power, and had to take prisoners as much as sixty miles to have them tried before civilian judges for petty offences. District magistrates also created problems by attempting to give unauthorized orders to police, there being no clear division of authority such as existed in India between the power of police officers and that of magistrates. This seemed particularly irritating to former members of the Royal North West Mounted Police, law officers who in Canada had the powers of justices of the peace. Yet in most respects the Canadian experience proved valuable. Steele noted that no efforts were being made to harvest hay, which necessitated importing forage for horses. He thereupon secured harvesting machines from North

America, a move which enabled the S.A.C. to procure forage from local sources. Even more useful was Steele's experience in the Yukon during the gold rush of 1898, when gold was discovered in the Latabra Hills in 1902. He rushed police to the scene, setting up registration offices and providing regulations for behaviour in the fields before the gold rush got underway. The S.A.C. was also charged with taking censuses, and later preparing election lists. By this time the force's intelligence service had reached a point where it could dismiss with confidence rumours of Kaffir uprisings, and give assurance that meetings of the Boer Het Volk party had no purpose more sinister than playing the political game and winning elections.

The greatest test of the S.A.C. came with the disastrous attempt of the mining interest to work their sites with imported Chinese contract labour. Protests at once arose in Britain that the policy amounted to importing slave labour. In South Africa, Boer, Kaffir and police alike saw the Chinese as a security problem. The Chinese were recruited by contractors who had no hesitation in drawing on prisons and the underworld in general in their search for workers. The latter in any case found themselves kept in inhospitable if not prison-like compounds by employers who called the roll once a week. Being in many cases highly skilled labourers capable of using dynamite which was available in the mines, some of the Chinese fabricated bombs, while out of bits and pieces of iron they fashioned knives and even two-handed swords. One of the more imaginative of their number even made maps which showed what was supposed to be a land route back to China.

Once outside the compounds they preyed on the Kaffir and Boer populations. When caught they usually insisted that they were simply on their way back to China. There moreover existed among them criminal secret societies which operated with a high degree of sophistication demonstrated in, for example, the case of the murder of a Boer farmer named Joubert. He had caught and turned in members of the Red Lantern Society. In revenge they sent several others of their number not closely linked to those turned in by Joubert, to carry out the killing. This same practice of using not closely or obviously implicated members of secret societies to carry out acts of revenge was practiced by the Irish Molly Maguires in the Pennsylvania coalfields in the 1870s. But in any event the Chinese in South Africa soon became a major problem as families abandoned homes in fear of raids. Steele's police patrols did their best but there was no real security until the use of Chinese labour was abolished in 1906.

With the reduction of the S.A.C. the same year that Chinese contract labour ceased, Steele returned to Canada. Altogether there had been over a thousand Canadians in the force, but it was not a completely happy story. Although at least half of them were immigrants to Canada, they insisted on serving together in their own exclusively Canadian units. On Steele's recommendation substantial numbers were placed in his division but apart from a troop of one hundred there were no solely Canadian formations as such. Many Canadian recruits who made good soldiers nonetheless proved unfit for police duties. There was among them as in the rest of the force a large turn-over.

The S.A.C. contribution to South African national reconciliation is best symbolized by the two hundred troopers who in 1904 formed the guard of honour at the state funeral of the Boer president, Paul Kruger. They were commanded by Colonel Sam Steele.

With the creation of the Union of South Africa in 1910 the various police forces, the S.A.C., Cape Mounted Rifles, Natal Mounted Police and others, were welded into a single unit. This process was complete by April 1913 when the South African Police came into being. This was a national police force responsible through its commissioner to the ministers of justice, police, and pensions. A separate government controlled Railway Police came into being in 1916 with jurisdiction over railways and harbours, and later airports. In 1937 they became an independent force under the ministry of transport. With the proliferation of motor cars, traffic control got too big for the South African Police. In 1937 municipal police took over traffic direction, and highway patrol became the responsibility of the four provincial governments, Cape Province, Transvaal, Orange Free State and Natal.

In South Africa all police functions were at times overshadowed by relations between the European minority and black majority. Consequently all forces were mixed forces, though until just recently the higher ranks have been exclusively European. Of these Baden-Powell's S.A.C. was the most interesting, and during its relatively short existence the most effective. It was of course temporary, and intended to be temporary. Yet Baden-Powell's achievement, like that of the Fielding brothers, remains an example of what can be accomplished when an acute and well-disposed intelligence begins to think about police work. Baden-Powell's achievement can provide useful lessons for future peace-keeping forces.

CHAPTER IX

RURAL AMERICA AND THE WILD WEST

URAL AMERICA MANAGED TO PRESERVE several English mediaeval police institutions down to the twentieth century. This is most noticeable in the enduring significance of the sheriff and the *posse comitatus*, which lost much of their importance in England with the emergence of the justice of the peace in the fourteenth century. In the more orderly eastern and, on the whole, northern regions of the British American colonies small homogeneous villages could without serious consequence remain in essence self-policing. In the south and in the west the police vacuum led to the rise of vigilantism and lynch law. The root cause of these phenomena was the inability, and in some cases the unwillingness, of law enforcement agencies to effectively do their duty, combined with the failure of the courts to impose penalties which the public thought suited the crimes committed. Many lynchings were carried out against those already incarcerated, on the assumption that the courts would not award adequate punishment. The practice flourished because of the widespread rationale that, if obviously guilty criminals could enjoy immunity from proper legal accountability, so too could self-appointed informal law enforcers who acted with a higher moral purpose to protect the community.

The practice of informal law enforcement antedates the American Revolution as the "Regulators" of South Carolina, a species of nightriders, imposed their own rules on the otherwise unpoliced frontier. By the same token, Indians accused of depredation against whites were murdered in their cells in west Pennsylvania in the decade before the revolution. The origin of the term "lynch law" is a matter of controversy, but some trace it back to a James Fitzstephen Lynch, warden of County Galway in Ireland. There are other candidates, principally a Colonel Charles Lynch who imposed informal so-called "justice" on suspected Loyalists on the Virginia frontier during the revolution. As his victims threatened to sue, a special act of indemnity was passed by the Virginia legislature, granting him immunity for alleged crimes, hence the phrase lynch law. Colonel Lynch, however, was content to have his victims beaten, and he did not impose the death penalty. Lynching, frequently of a much more lethal character, was a phenomenon of the frontier expected to perish with it, until the agitation of abolitionists and the Nat Turner slave rebellion of 1831 created a visceral fear in the south.

There followed an outbreak of informal "law" enforcement directed mainly against white abolitionists and blacks — the latter both slaves and freemen — with known or suspected intentions against the established order of white supremacy, but also sometimes encompassing a wide range of other, non-racial, offenders who could on occasion be found in most any community. By about 1833 the word "lynch" became the accepted term for such informal law enforcement. Examples of the application of lynch law directed against abolitionists occurred in the north also at this time, but these did not reach anything like the same proportions as in the states below the Mason-Dixon line. While in the south blacks considered to have committed serious crime — including abolition-related activity — usually suffered a violent death, frequently being tortured in the process and sometimes burned alive as a special deterrent, for white abolitionists the more standard punishment was the lash or tar and feathers, though some white anti-slavery agitators were murdered also. However, in a few instances where the identities of mob participants were known, surviving victims successfully sued for damages, and "lynch" was still not necessarily synonymous with killing in the way it, for good reason, soon became so.

This lawlessness continued after the Civil War when, during the Reconstruction period, Radical Republicans together with their scalawag and carpetbagger associates controlled the ex-Confederate state governments by using for the most part ill-educated blacks (including voters, legislature members and other officials) as pawns while they punished and exploited the largely disfranchised white population. Southern whites, some of them members of the pre-war Knights of the Golden Circle secret society, responded with renewed vigilantism, most notably under the auspices of the Ku Klux Klan, first organized in 1867 in Pulaski, Tennessee, under the leadership of former Confederate officer Nathan Bedford Forrest. With its burning cross motif descended from the traditional rallying beacon of Scotland's Highland clans, as well as its own distinctive masked and hooded regalia, its parades, fantastic ranks, cere-monies and doctrine of the "Invisible Empire," the Klan under a variety of leaders and with sometimes competing branches has been easily the most colourful and "public" of American nativist, white supremacist societies.

Apart from the south, vigilantism remained basically a fron-tier phenomenon which filled a police vacuum. Most efforts to oth-erwise fill this vacuum proved either inadequate or total failures.

A vigilance court (from *Harper's Weekly*, April 11th, 1874).

There was no really widely effective solution found to frontier policing, which was on the whole left in the first instance to the settlers and in the last to the military. The most successful local police effort to deal with the frontier problem was the Texas Rangers, who have acquired an on the whole well-deserved name in history and folklore. The term "ranger" seems to be derived from seventeenth century Scotland, where it designated armed men who patrolled the borders of a clan's territory to prevent the theft of live-stock and give warning of raids by hostile neighbours. The word arrived in America by 1739, for in that year Governor George Oglethorpe of Georgia raised a troop called the Highland Rangers.

The practice caught on and within a decade or two nearly all the colonies had organized ranger companies. In the course of

A nineteenth century
U.S. sheriff.

the mid-eighteenth century wars with the French and their Indian allies (especially the Abenaki), Major Robert Rogers, a New Hampshireman of Ulster antecedents, raised a body of woods-wise, fast-travelling and hard-fighting frontiersmen skilled in the methods of guerrilla warfare. Though they never numbered more than a few hundred at any one time, these green-clad troops became well known in colonial America as Rogers' Rangers, their most famous exploit doubtless being the 1759 punitive expedition deep into New France which destroyed the Abenaki stronghold of St. Francis (Odanak) at the confluence of the St. Francis and St. Lawrence Rivers. Though in reality the St. Francis raid proved something of a pyrrhic victory, Rogers' Rangers subsequently acquired a certain immortality, not least because of their role in Kenneth Roberts' novel *Northwest Passage* and a Hollywood film of the same name. But in any case, by 1800 ranger regiments existed in the British regular forces, the best known being the Connaught Rangers who achieved a distinguished record during the Peninsular War.

While Texas was still a province of New Spain, American frontiersmen were invited to settle there and develop the land. After independence the Mexican government authorized these settlers — the vast majority from the southern states, and some of them slave-holders — to provide a small body of armed men to deal with Indian raids. Hence the "rangers," at first in fact known by various other names also, came into existence a mere ten strong in 1823. Over the years they developed into an irregular force of several companies under paid captains, each ranger providing his own horse and weapons with no fixed period of service. They played a minor part in the Texas War of Independence from Mexico (1835-1836), but were established by the fledgling Republic of Texas as a permanent body consisting of three companies of fifty-six men, each commanded by a captain assisted by a first and second lieutenant under the over-all command of a major. Although referred to as serving in battalions, with their officers holding military rank, the Texas Rangers remained in every sense irregulars. They still provided their own horses and weapons, and wore no uniforms. They travelled light, often living off the land by hunting and not bothering to employ pack horses or wagons. At a rate of $1.25 a day, theirs was probably the highest salary for police in the world at the time. In every sense frontiersmen, they acquired the habits of their enemies, and some of them took Indian scalps until at least the 1870s.

Ranger officers tended to be men of strong personality, indeed what might be termed "characters." Their first major, Robert Williamson, originally a Georgian, was a district judge who prominently agitated against Mexican authority prior to the outbreak of open rebellion in 1835. Williamson had a leg so badly crippled by polio that he walked with a wooden replacement from the knee down, being known to his fellow Rangers as "three-legged Willie." Captain Jack Hays, from Tennessee, was another personality, with the distinction of introducing the Colt revolver to the force and thus greatly increasing its fire-power in close range fighting. The initial model so employed was the five-shot Colt Patterson, a weapon which used the new percussion cap ignition system and constituted the world's first successful revolver when it appeared in 1836.

It took some time to become readily available on the frontier, but Hays demonstrated the Patterson's worth in 1844 when, in command of fourteen men, he encountered on the Pedernales River a raiding party of some seventy Comanche Indians, members of the most formidable tribe then in regular hostile contact with Texans. When the Rangers discharged their muzzle-loading single-shot rifles, the Indians charged, assuming that Hays and his men,

A border patrol in Texas.

having no time to reload, could be overwhelmed by numerical superiority. But much to their surprise, Hays instructed his much smaller force to "Powder-burn them!" and ordered a counter-charge. Faced with the novelty of repeating handguns at close quarters, the Comanches broke, leaving thirty dead on the field. The Colt Patterson was soon replaced by an improved though heavy six-shot weapon on the initiative of another Ranger person-ality, Samuel H. Walker, who induced the inventive gun-designer Samuel Colt to produce what became known as the Colt Walker.

With the defeat of Mexican authority and the creation of an independent Republic of Texas in 1836, the Rangers began to win a place in history and folklore. They long remained, however, pri-marily frontier Indian fighters, and were not used to maintain inter-nal order. For example they were not called on to deal with the feud between the "Regulators" and "Moderators" which disrupted Selby County between 1840 and 1844, a matter which required the intervention of the militia. During the United States' Mexican War (1845-1848) the Rangers played a conspicuous part as scouts not only with General Zachary Taylor's army which invaded Mexico from the north, but also General Winfield Scott's seaborne expedition which landed at Vera Cruz. During these campaigns Rangers proved useful out of all proportion to their numbers, and they alone, not the American regular forces, successfully countered Mexican guerrillas. They reputedly took no prisoners — perhaps not especially surprising in view of their backgrounds as Indian fighters who also remembered the Alamo and Goliad, not forgetting several Mexican slaughters of captured Texans in the early 1840s — while their habit of shooting noncombatants who shouted abuse at them led Scott to send them away from Mexico City.

With the end of the Mexican War in 1848, the Rangers were for a short time almost disbanded. Walker had been killed in action during the recent conflict, and Hays left for California during the gold rush. However, public protest about the inefficiency of the U.S. regular army as Indian fighters brought about a restoration of the Texas Rangers in the form of three companies in 1849, which grew to six in 1852. In that year half the complement were assigned to the southern frontier for border patrol, and for a brief time efforts to secure federal funding met with some success. When this came to an end in 1854 the Rangers once more became a purely state force. Not that their reputation remained confined to Texas, however; and, doubtless in tribute to fellow southerners, personnel of at least one pro-slavery mounted unit fighting the Free Soil forces in contemporary "Bleeding Kansas" apparently took to styling themselves Kansas Rangers.

In any case, the Texas Rangers enjoyed some advantages over the U.S. regulars who, being under orders from Washington, could not cross the border whereas Rangers, caring nothing for diplomatic distinctions in matters of life and death, showed no hesitation in crossing the frontier after Indians, bandits or anyone else even if it involved clashes with Mexican troops. This came to the fore when, in 1859, the Mexican General Juan Cortina sought to launch an Hispanic rebellion in the Brownsville area. Though the Rangers suffered an initial defeat, they in conjunction with the U.S. cavalry soon drove Cortina back into Mexico. The Texans as usual crossed the border in pursuit but this time were prevailed upon to return by the moral authority of the new local regular army officer in charge, Colonel Robert E. Lee. The latter figure would, indeed, soon return to his native Virginia, where he proved instrumental in the capture of the extreme abolitionist, John Brown, who raided the federal arsenal at Harper's Ferry to procure arms for an intended slave rebellion. Thereafter Lee went on to win a legendary place in American history during the Civil War as the commander of that most storied of Confederate forces, the Army of Northern Virginia, which included some Texas infantry regiments but evidently no notable number of ex-Ranger horsemen amongst its cavalry.

Texas seceded with the rest of the slave states early in 1861, and during the Civil War the Rangers, while formally still in existence, again all but totally faded away as men of military age and ability focused their attention on the internecine national conflict. Many former Texas Ranger personnel served as Confederate cavalry or mounted rifles, especially in the "local" Trans-Mississippi Department, though being subject to army regulation and orders they no longer functioned as traditional Rangers. One such Confederate mounted unit was called the Partisan Rangers; another, Terry's Rangers, in honour of the surname of its commanding officer, but there do not appear to have been any southern military formations with the Texas Rangers appellation as such. A special Frontier Battalion of old men and boys, nominal Rangers who attempted to fill the role of "real" ones, was unable to prevent the Comanches from raiding outlying settlements along a hundred mile front.

Moreover, while vigilantism was even in what passed for more normal times a fact of life in Texas, an area which signally blended characteristics of the south and the west, the coming of the Civil War did nothing to discourage the practice of lynching, or raise the standard of internal policing. Speaking of this period, Robert Hamilton Williams in his *With the Border Ruffians* memoirs records the cynicism and callousness with which John Atkins, a member of the dreaded San Antonio Vigilance Committee, after several days' show of camaraderie on the trail with a young man in custody named Jack Young, had the prisoner hanged outside town because a fair trial might have acquitted him of the charge of stealing Atkins' horse. Williams, who with experience in the Kansas Rangers, Confederate Partisan Rangers and as an Indian fighter participated in his share of violence, nonetheless remained for the rest of his life particularly shocked by the Young incident. As he put it, "I have, alas! seen many die by Lynch Law, but never so cold-blooded a deed as this one." Significantly, when the outraged Williams reported the killing, the San Antonio city marshal, completely under the sway of the local Vigilance Committee, refused to proceed against Atkins and his companions for murder. He indeed did nothing beyond sending a party of Mexicans to cut Young's body down and bury the man where he died. It would be difficult to imagine a more complete surrender to illegal authority by an officer sworn to uphold legally constituted authority and due process of law, but such pusillanimous behaviour was not unique to this San Antonio marshal of the early 1860s.

Despite the unusually disturbed condition of society, with the end of the war what little remained of the Texas Rangers, basically just the Frontier Battalion, was once more disbanded. They stayed dormant until 1873, when the Reconstruction period came to an end. At that point the Democratic state government authorized six new Texas Ranger companies — these, initially, primarily for border patrol because the boundary with Mexico remained a trouble spot due to banditry, though the Indian frontier had for the most part moved farther west. Yet at the same time there came increased recognition of the need to effectively deal with serious, chronic domestic disorders marked by cattle and horse rustling, now accompanied by the feuds of competing ranching interests. All this was further complicated by lingering bitterness between Democrats and Republicans arising out of the Civil War and, especially, the Reconstruction era.

To meet these problems a further re-organization took place in 1874, whereby the reconstituted Rangers were divided into a Frontier Battalion under Major John B. Jones; and a Special Force, to deal with the problem of internal disorder, commanded by Captain Leander H. McNelly who became the leading Ranger personality during the next few years. After fighting for the south in Louisiana, McNelly had commanded in Texas one of the last Confederate military units to lay down its arms at the end of the Civil War. Despite this he subsequently, during the Reconstruction years, served in the extremely unpopular Radical Republican-sponsored State Police, a fact which the new Democratic administration was in its turn prepared to overlook. McNelly's iron hand kept the Rangers under strict control while they suppressed vigilantism on the American side of the line and made frequent border crossings in pursuit of bandits on the other.

In 1877 tuberculosis forced McNelly to relinquish his command to Lieutenant Lee Hall, under whose leadership the Texas Rangers took some preliminary steps towards being a more conventional, bureaucratic police force: for example, keeping and concentrating on a formal statewide list of suspects, rather than hunting for criminals by relying mostly on "instinct" and the lessons of frontier experience. But life remained for a time yet substantially a matter of individual exploits and personal initiative, with recourse to firearms not uncommon. This changed further with the turn of the century, however, as the Rangers were thereafter increasingly left with the routine duties of state police. Appointments became more obviously political than before, and special commissions were sometimes given to patently dubious individuals with friends in the right places. Reform came in 1934 when the force, without changing its name, was transformed into a state bureau of investigation. In this new role the Rangers lost the last vestiges of the romance of the frontier, but still retained their importance in Texas.

When former Ranger Jack Hays moved west to the gold fields of California he brought his reputation with him, finding himself elected sheriff of San Francisco at the same time the city was incorporated in 1850. Yet he did not bring the Texas Rangers with him, nor did he make an effort to create a similar institution on the west coast. McNelly, a generation later, might have been able to cope with the prevailing Californian conditions by using his Special Force, but Hays remained essentially an Indian fighter and Indians were not the problem.

On the gold fields no police existed; hence the miners organized their own councils and enforced law as they understood it. There were likewise no jail facilities, so banishment, flogging and hanging presented themselves as the only possible penalties. Repeated offences, even minor ones, frequently brought the death penalty, such being the case not only in San Francisco but throughout the west. San Francisco itself was terrorized by a group known as the "Hounds" who paraded with a brass band and, looting and killing, victimized Hispanics especially. The answer to the Hounds proved to be not Hays but vigilantes, the initiative being taken by Samuel Brannan, the editor of the city's first newspaper. On the 16th of July 1850 Brannan called a public meeting and, regardless of threats by the Hounds, demanded action against the group. They were accordingly rounded up and tried in an improvised court, a process which lasted several days. Next followed a sentence of banishment from the city, after which the crowds that brought them to justice disbanded.

But as the population of San Francisco boomed to almost fifty thousand, criminals from all over the world migrated to the locale, some of the most notorious being runaways from the penal colonies across the Pacific in Australia. Brannan again took the lead in forming a public vigilante committee. They adopted a constitution announcing their intention to restore law and order, soon apprehended an Australian named John Jenkins while he was robbing a safe. After the volunteer fire department bell collected a crowd, Jenkins was tried and convicted by a vigilante court with more or less regular judicial procedures being followed. The verdict was immediate execution. A noose was placed around Jenkins' neck, the rope thrown over a beam, and members of the assembled crowd seized the rope and Jenkins duly hanged. Following this there occurred a general clean up of "undesirables," many being forcefully deported while others thought it best to leave on their own. From that time on the vigilante committee took upon themselves the function of immigration officers and particularly closely monitored all those arriving from Australia.

The second hanging involved another Australian, James Stuart. Although a defence lawyer secured a writ of *habeas corpus* which he took to Sheriff Hays, no serious effort was made to rescue Stuart, soon executed in the same manner as Jenkins. Formal protests ensued from the mayor of San Francisco and the governor of California condemning the procedure, but a grand jury refused to indict those held responsible. Similar scenes were enacted throughout the state and indeed throughout the west. In some cases vigilance committees would arrest suspects and turn them over to the formal legal authorities, but when they believed acquittal or too light penalties would result, they imposed their own idea of justice. Such proved true in the instances of yet two more Australians, Samuel Whittaker and Robert McKenzie, at first seized by vigilantes, then on the insistence of the governor taken into regular custody by a reluctant Sheriff Hays. The outraged vigilantes thereupon attacked the jail, seized the criminals, rang the by now customary bell to assemble a crowd, and hanged Whittaker and McKenzie. This took place in 1851, after which there followed four years of relative quiet.

But in 1855 the shooting of an unarmed U.S. marshal by Charles Cora reanimated the vigilantes. Brannan again called for action, but the public was at first prepared to let the law take its course. Cora's case was discharged by a "hung" jury, whereupon James Casey, a local machine politician, shot and mortally wounded James King, a newspaper editor who had been exposing jury-tampering and related corruption surrounding the Cora trial. The vigilantes again assembled while militiamen were called out to protect Casey and Cora, now both in custody. Yet in spite of the militia they were surrendered to the vigilantes. As their trial by the vigilantes proceeded news came of the death of the wounded editor, James King. To avoid possible rescue, Casey and Cora were hanged during King's funeral. While this proved the last episode of vigilantism in San Francisco, the practice survived where conditions warranted for another several generations elsewhere in the west with vigilantes, sometimes openly supported by the press and prominent citizens, in other instances acting secretly as nightriders, continuing to flourish.

The root cause of vigilante action lay in the failure of the two principal law enforcement officials, the sheriff and the marshal, to function effectively. A few holders of these positions, like "Wild Bill" Hickock and Wyatt Earp, gained a conspicuous place in western lore; but the office of sheriff or marshal carried only as much real authority as the incumbent could impose by his personality, and by his prowess with weapons. The choice for communities seemed to be between acceptance of organized crime and the dominance of local bullies, or the taking of the law into one's own hands — both very primitive options — or, again, more civilized and regular recourse to duly authorized law officers. As for the latter, sheriffs were elected locally at the county or town level; marshals could be either elected at the municipal level, or appointed by municipal, state or federal government.

James Hickock, known as "Wild Bill" Hickock, one of the most famous marshals, proved in reality to be something less than the paragon of the frontier virtues he has sometimes been depicted. Rather dandified, though fearless and an expert shot, in 1871 he found himself dismissed from office as marshal of Abilene, Kansas, when he killed a bystander as well as his intended opponent during a gun fight sparked by a personal feud. Thereafter Hickock for a time toured with a theatrical troupe, and met his end in Deadwood, Dakota Territory, when shot in the back during a saloon poker game in 1876. The next year another notable lawman came to the fore when William ("Bat") Masterson was elected sheriff of Dodge City, Kansas, his older brother Edward Masterson acting as deputy marshal, and both men having recently acted there as deputies of Wyatt Earp. Distinguished by the fine cut of his clothes and a dapper demeanour, Bat Masterson was nonetheless a deadly shot who maintained reasonable law and order in difficult circumstances. Though his brother died in the line of duty, Bat survived his career in the west, eventually moving on to work as a sports writer in New York City.

Perhaps the best known of the western lawmen-cum-gunfighters was Wyatt Earp, whose part in the exploits at the O.K. Corral have been the subject of at least three films. Earp, a mustached teeto-

Wild Bill Hickok.

taller in a generally hard-drinking setting, stood over six feet tall, and began making his reputation in 1876 as chief deputy marshal of Dodge City where he earned $250 per year, plus $2.50 for every arrest. After a stint in Deadwood, Earp returned to Dodge City as marshal in 1878 where he in a sense up-staged Bat Masterson who failed in his attempted re-election as sheriff. But it was Earp's years in Tombstone, Arizona that really brought him to public attention nationally. Arriving there as deputy sheriff late in 1879, Earp found employment with the Wells Fargo Express Company and also had a quarter interest in a gambling house called the *Oriental* which brought him a large income apart from his sometime work as a law officer.

Tension arose between Earp and the Clantons and McLowerys, local ranching families with underworld associations whose activities the elected sheriff tolerated. A citizens' committee finally demanded action and made Wyatt Earp, his two brothers Virgil and Morgan, and their friend John ("Doc") Holliday their agents. The Clantons and McLowerys responded with threats, following which Ike Clanton, the most belligerent and leader of the band, was in October 1881 arrested, fined, and told to leave town. This he did but returned the next day. Then, with more threats against the Earps and Holliday, and after considerable drinking, Ike Clanton and his men gathered at the local O.K. Corral. Virgil Earp, who held office as marshal, informed the sheriff that he intended to arrest the Clantons and their associates. The sheriff consented but refused to accompany the Earps and Holliday to what promised to be a violent confrontation. There followed in Tombstone one of the classic gunfights in the history of the American west, a shoot-out at the O.K. Corral in which William Clanton and two McLowerys were killed. Virgil and Morgan Earp and Doc Holliday suffered slight injuries. Quiet descended on Tombstone but many area inhabitants, even those with no partiality for the Earps' enemies, saw the affair as too much of a personal quarrel with drunken toughs rather than completely even-handed law enforcement.

On the whole the sheriff and marshal throughout the west had difficulty in keeping free of local politics and local feuds. In any case they could usually offer little protection for those with valuable property to protect. This task fell to private organizations, the most famous being the Pinkerton Detective Agency founded by Alan Pinkerton. Born in 1819 in Glasgow, Scotland, where his father had been a policeman, young Pinkerton became an active Chartist and, after his arrival in America, an abolitionist. He was originally a cooper by trade, who served as a part-time deputy sheriff in a suburb of Chicago where he proved effective in dealing with an outbreak of counterfeiting. This led to a temporary appointment by the U.S. treasury in 1851-1853. In the latter year he became a special agent for the U.S. post office and at the same time founded his own railway police agency. Railways had a particular need for private agencies of this sort because no city, county, state or federal police were prepared to give them adequate protection. Once beyond city limits, trains and their cargoes were on their own.

Initially most of Pinkerton's work involved checking the honesty of railway employees. Professional police arrived late in Chicago (1855), when the city's inadequate security left the ground clear for a former county sheriff, Cyrus Bradley, to organize a highly profitable private police. Pinkerton did the same in 1858 and his firm was soon given power of arrest. During the Civil War, Pinkerton employees performed secret service work. They did this for the most part quite successfully, their major defeat being the failure to prevent the assassination of President Abraham Lincoln by John Wilkes Booth at Ford's Theatre in Washington. Some of the most remarkable work of the agency involved dealing with train robbers. Not only did they in this connection pursue the Missourian Jesse James and his ex-Confederate guerrilla associates, but they waged a determined campaign against the Renos, a criminal family based in Jackson County, Indiana.

Originally named Renault, probably of Huguenot descent, the Renos numbered six: Frank, John, Simeon, Clinton, William, and Laura Ellen. Being by the early Civil War years already in the opinion of their neighbours guilty of arson and other criminality, the Reno brothers left Jackson County suddenly for fear of nightriders. They then joined the Union forces for the bounty money, promptly deserting and re-enlisting under other identities. At the end of the war their notoriety continued as they turned to train robbery, and hence became a target for the Pinkertons. In all cases of breaking up organized bands of criminals, Pinkerton's basic method was infiltration. In this instance his agent, Richard Winscott, opened a conveniently located bar which, as calculated, soon attracted the patronage of the Renos. Winning their confidence, Winscott managed to secure a photograph of two of the family, John and Frank. It being deemed futile and dangerous to attempt to arrest them on their home ground, a decision was made to kidnap them. To effect this they were induced to come to a railway station some distance away to wait for a "friend." Six Pinkerton agents arrived on a special train, identified John Reno from the photo, seized him and took him aboard as they moved out of the station. Reno pleaded guilty and was sentenced to twenty-five years in prison.

Frank Reno then assumed leadership of the gang, whose criminal activities and bad reputation exceeded previous limits. Frank was captured briefly by Pinkerton men but escaped from the county jail in April 1868. In a related connection, several other apprehended bandits being escorted to prison by the Pinkertons were, together with their lawful captors, surrounded by an overwhelming force of particularly determined nightriders called Red Masks. The latter without further ado hanged the Pinkertons' prisoners. Only a few days after this, William and Simeon Reno found themselves in turn arrested and taken to the county jail. In view of the immediate threat that the Red Masks would raid the facility and lynch the two men, the county accepted the offer of Laura Ellen Reno to pay the expense of transporting her brothers to a more secure prison at New Albany, in Floyd County. This being unknown to the Red Masks, they and a crowd of several hundred supporters launched a well-organized attack on Lexington Prison, which the Renos had just left. Their quarry having eluded them, they then blockaded the railway, hoping to find the men on a train, but the two Renos had been taken to New Albany by boat.

Meanwhile Frank Reno, two of his brothers, and their associate Charles Anderson took refuge in Windsor, Ontario. There they were apprehended and, after the intervention of the governor general, extradited on the understanding that they would be tried by due process in the United States. In a sense they thus enjoyed an international guarantee, but the relentless Red Mask vigilantes could not be expected to show any concern for the niceties of diplomacy. When it became known that the Renos had been returned to New Albany, threats to lynch them met counter-threats against the vigilantes from the Renos' underworld associates. Every reason existed to place the jail under military protection, as the building was declared to be unsafe by a local committee. But nothing was done in this regard, and at midnight on the 11th of December 1868 the Red Masks commandeered a train, cut the telegraph wires, and set off for New Albany.

Arriving at 3 a.m., they took command of the main street of the town and overcame the lone, sleeping guard in immediate charge of the Renos. The local sheriff was then severely beaten, the vigilantes threatening to burn the jail with the prisoners in it if the lawman still refused to disclose the hiding place of the keys.

The keys finally were found and the three Reno brothers Frank, William and Simeon, together with Charles Anderson, hanged without further delay. The sensational character of the story made it a feature even in the *Times* of London, while the embarrassed U.S. secretary of state publicly apologized to the British government for the triumph of Red Mask vigilante justice over the due process of law.

The Reno drama was a few years later surpassed by the better known case of the Molly Maguires. Alan Pinkerton until this time refused to have anything to do with divorce cases, or strikes and labour disputes. In his youth he had been a man of the left as a Chartist and abolitionist. Although his agents previously protected employers against fraud by employees, Pinkerton's decision to act against the Mollys represented something new.

The Molly Maguires were a self-constituted terrorist society affiliated with the large and respectable Ancient Order of Hibernians. They took the oaths and used the passwords of the Hibernians, but acted entirely on their own, bringing to the post-Civil War Pennsylvania coal fields a primitive and violent type of unionism which adopted the means of the agrarian secret societies they or their immediate forebears knew in Ireland. There was, indeed, much justice in the cause they championed. In 1871 alone a hundred and twelve men died in mining accidents, with three hundred and thirty-nine permanently incapacitated by injuries. Company stores overcharged miners, while cheap labour periodically imported from Continental Europe set limits to what strike action could accomplish. Moreover there existed little prospect of impartial law enforcement, as the state sold commissions in the Coal and Iron Police for $1.00 to appointees of the mine owners. Under such conditions the Mollys hit back by the methods used against Irish landlords, murdering selected company managers and associated officers. These, at the most immediate level of contact, were largely Welsh Protestants and as such, even apart from the fact that they represented the mine owners' interests, not much prone to sympathy with their Irish Catholic fellow immigrants. Like their Chinese counterparts a generation later in South Africa, the Irish miners adopted the practice of assigning local murders to distant members of their secret society.

Alan Pinkerton accepted the challenge of breaking up the Molly Maguires on the grounds that they were guilty of terrorism and murder. As in the precedent of the Reno family, his main method was infiltration. He found a very able agent for the purpose in James MacPharlan, whose ability to plausibly sing Irish rebel songs and dance a jig helped him ingratiate himself with the coal miners. MacPharlan, under the suitably Irish name of McKenna, gained the miners' confidence, following which he did his best to frustrate plans to assassinate various company officials but did not succeed in all instances. Pinkerton difficulties increased when John Kehoe, the principal Molly Maguire leader, won election as a chief constable. Matters were further complicated by an outbreak of vigilantism which killed the wife of a Molly Maguire gunman. MacPharlan, not without a sense of decency, was outraged by this conduct and threatened to resign though, the Pinkerton agency had no part in the woman's death. In the end the arrest of a killer secretly exposed by MacPharlan made Kehoe suspicious. The Pinkerton agent was accordingly marked for execution, but managed to pull out in time, and escape with his life.

The Molly Maguires soon passed into folklore. Sir Arthur Conan Doyle wrote a novel, *The Valley of Fear*, in which the Pinkerton man is the hero, while some labour historians have seen the Mollys as a laudable manifestation of class struggle. Likewise, a Hollywood film called *The Molly Maguires* portrayed their cause sympathetically. Theirs was undoubtedly a protest against exploitation, but it also involved more than protest, particularly the ambitions of a leader like Kehoe. Apart from this, the Mollys brought with them the habits of conspiracy against authority from rural Ireland, which served both as a means of protest and a way of life. The murder of individual representatives of the coal company system was more likely to provoke vigilantism than to further the Mollys' interests, however, and the Pinkertons at least ensured that only gunmen guilty of murder suffered prosecution. Vigilante reprisals, in contrast, tended to be indiscriminate attacks on the whole Irish coal mining community. Alan Pinkerton considered the Mollys as being on the same level as the Ku Klux Klan in that they were conspirators who took the law into their own hands, and thus became fair game for his agency.

The central difficulty was the lack of any effective U.S. secret service capable of dealing with conspiratorial groups. The treasury department maintained a secret service of sorts to deal with counterfeiting which, as previously noted, at one point employed young Alan Pinkerton. But most such treasury agents were hired from approved private detective agencies on a part-time basis only, and in any event the focus of their activity was narrow. It was Attorney General Charles Bonaparte, descended from a brother of Napoleon, who in 1907 made a plea for an organized U.S. secret service. It took nothing less than the intervention of President Theodore Roosevelt to provide the attorney general with an investigative force which came into being in 1908 and is today known as the Federal Bureau of Investigation (F.B.I.), a federal agency with authority to go anywhere in the United States.

The first great challenge to the secret service came in World War I. With some assistance from British intelligence and Allied sympathizers, the largely inept schemes of German agents were nearly all defeated in the years leading up to the American declaration of war in April 1917. American secret service then faced what appeared to be the formidable task of monitoring one million enemy aliens with a force of only three hundred. There could be no question of interning such a large number but investigation was necessary, and by the end of the war six thousand three hundred had been arrested, though only two thousand three hundred interned. In reality it was not German agents or sympathizers, but fear of them, which proved the great problem. The Espionage Act was amended to include subversive activities as self-appointed patriots began spying on their neighbours. At the same time, Councils for Defence undertook to issue warnings to those whom they considered suspect, insisting that the accused clear themselves before the same self-appointed council.

Efforts of the attorney general to secure public cooperation led to the sponsoring of the American Protective League, a group of volunteer unpaid aides to security which grew to number two hundred thousand, each member being given a badge and a certificate. Most simply took the badge and did nothing, but a nucleus of busybodies and fanatics assumed the power of arrest and the right to search. Civil rights were ignored, and some employers used the

more extreme elements of the American Protective League to intimi-
date strikers. The public in any case had difficulty distinguishing
between political opponents of the war like the Industrial Workers of
the World (I.W.W.), and German agents. In one instance a member
of the I.W.W. was murdered by masked vigilantes in Butte,
Montana, after which President Woodrow Wilson publicly warned
against "taking the law into one's own hands." Meanwhile the
I.W.W. leader, William Heywood, and the head of the Socialist party,
Eugene Debs, found themselves arrested, tried and imprisoned. At
the same time a campaign was launched against draft evaders, estimated to number over three hundred thousand. In a sweep using
police, military and Protective League members, fifty thousand men
were detained in the New York City area alone in September 1918,
mostly those of military age who were not carrying draft cards. Of
these, only about fifteen thousand actually were draft delinquents
and an outcry resulted in the press; but the policy would probably
have continued had the war not ended in November 1918.

With the overseas conflict finished the need remained for an
enemy, and the radical movement became the new target. This was
not altogether without provocation as some I.W.W. members had
employed terrorism. Moreover, parties unknown bombed and nearly
killed Attorney General A. Mitchell Palmer and his wife on the 2nd of
June 1919. Bombs and inflammatory literature spread by small
groups claiming to be revolutionary provided the background for the
excesses of the "Palmer raids," but the real difficulty was that the
government, lacking any effective professional secret service, was in
the dark. They could not distinguish between real conspiracies, mere
theorists, and social unrest. The study of revolutionary literature was
misleading because it provided only social analysis rather than conspiratorial plans. Given the fact of the Russian revolution and its
many sympathizers, it was easy to see the small and recently founded Communist groups as a cause rather than a result of social unrest.

In any event it would have been in the interest of radical
groups to be infiltrated by trained, politically sophisticated agents who
could have given the authorities assurance that such groups had no
immediate plans for a *coup d'état*. However, radical infiltration of
conventional organizations demanded supervision, for they were in
fact much later to provide recruiting grounds for real, as distinct from

imaginary, Soviet spies. Conspiratorial they were, but conspiracies have never been formidable against organized government. As an early twentieth century conspirator against the Tsar's police, Lenin was no more successful than Guy Fawkes against James I in early seventeenth century England. Lenin's victory was over Alexander Kerensky's chaotic democratic republic. What the Communists planned to do was to wait for, and when possible hasten, a general breakdown of society, then seize power. This intended scenario was not understood by casual readers of revolutionary literature, nor by those who talked with Soviet sympathizers. Suspicion of widespread Soviet conspiracy found further stimulation with the arrival in New York of Ludwig Martens as Soviet trade representative. He soon got in touch with American radicals, and reportedly had at his disposal some $ 200,000,000. In a sense this constituted a conspiracy, but in spite of their clandestine habits, the Communists planned to engage in legal activities. Had it not been for the bombing campaign, which was probably the work of anarchist splinter groups, there would have been no "red scare." As it was, the public demand for action brought about the so-called Palmer raids on various Communist organizations. In the course of the raids due process was neglected, which resulted in condemnation of the whole affair when public hysteria subsided.

There was no credit to be had for the F.B.I. in any of this, nor indeed much recognition of any kind until J. Edgar Hoover became head of the organization in 1928. At that time the various municipal and state authorities had lost control of the underworld. Hoover, with his gift for publicity, moved into the gap as a "gang-buster" and made the F.B.I. famous. Whatever his faults — and he has many critics — Hoover took a floundering federal secret service and turned it into a first-rate investigation bureau.

The American colonies, which separated from the crown at a time when Britain itself had no professional police, clung tenaciously to the rudimentary police institutions of mediaeval England. Professionalism was scorned as an un-American practice. Consequently the gap was filled by make-shift arrangements, sometimes by notable personalities like Wyatt Earp, in other cases by private police agencies like the Pinkertons. Yet all too often this opened the door to vigilantism and its consequent disregard for those liberties which professional police were supposed to endanger.

CHAPTER X

THE CANADIAN POLICE PERSPECTIVE

CANADA, IN GENERAL, FACED FEWER social problems than the United States did, with New France developing under a relatively bureaucratic regime and much of English Canada being settled at a later time when Britain itself was coming under bureaucratic government. There also existed no revolutionary tradition or mythology which made a particular virtue of resistance to authority. Moreover, the large military-to-civilian ratio provided Canada with a reserve of former soldiers who constituted potential policemen.

In secret service matters only temporary agents were employed before the outbreak of the American Civil War. At that time the need arose for intelligence with respect to Confederate agents in Canada, many of them escaped prisoners of war, planning border incursions and sabotage against the U.S. in violation of Britain's official neutrality in the conflict. Two detective forces were consequently organized. One, under Charles Coursol, a Montreal police magistrate, was based in that city; a second, directed by Sarnia Police Magistrate Gilbert McMicken, not only discreetly scrutinized local activities but maintained its own network of undercover informants in the United States. The Confederate issue disappeared with the end of the Civil War, only to be almost immediately replaced by the Irish American menace of cross-border Fenian raids. These then became the concern of McMicken's organization especially, aided by Edward Archibald, the British consul in New York, and H.W. Hemans, the consul at Buffalo.

The first crisis came in March 1866 as the Toronto St. Patrick's Day parade approached. Michael Murphy, the head of the city's Fenian-controlled Hibernian Society, insisted on holding the parade even as rumours circulated that Fenian incursions from the United States would be coordinated with a local Irish nationalist uprising. Any parade managed by the Hibernians posed a real threat of a major riot, but as McMicken's agent Patrick Nolan had infiltrated the society, the detective chief knew that no plans existed for an immediate rising. McMicken contacted Murphy who seemed genuinely alarmed at the prospect of a riot, yet was unwilling to back down. In a compromise, the two men agreed that the parade should proceed, though without any provocative party signs or insignia calculated to arouse the passions of the Orange and the Green factions in the city. Further, McMicken arranged for the militia, who included many potential rioters, to be called out and kept in their armouries during the parade while he and Orange Grand Master Ogle R. Gowan monitored the event. The latter transpired without violent incident, ending good-naturedly with three cheers for the Pope and the Queen.

Since Murphy belonged to the Fenian wing opposed to the invasion of Canada, at the moment his protests of loyalty to his new country were at least to that extent sincere. Yet unknown to him, on the very day of the parade the leadership of his Fenian faction in the United States changed their policy and decided to invade Canada after all. British and Canadian authorities learned of the decision at once, thanks to James "Red" MacDermott, an informant who sold the information to Edward Archibald, the British consul in New York. Murphy felt bound by the new policy when apprised of it, and was later arrested in Cornwall, presumably *en route* to join the Fenians gathered to attack Campobello Island, New Brunswick, from Maine. But with all chance of surprise gone and substantial British and Canadian forces on the scene, the assault when it came in April 1866 fizzled out in a futile gesture against not Campobello but a customs house on nearby Indian Island.

The Campobello fiasco produced a mood of complacency in both Canadian and British intelligence-gathering circles. Consequently the more formidable Fenian raid in Ontario's Niagara Peninsula caught the authorities completely by surprise when it issued in the Battles of Ridgeway and Fort Erie early in June of the same year. They were more fortunate with the Eccles Hill and Trout River incursions of May 1870 in Quebec, being well-informed through the reports of "Henri Le Caron," an adventurous Englishman whose real name was Michael Beach. Le Caron, at first a free-lance volunteer and then an officially if of course secretly employed British agent who liked to live very dangerously, infiltrated in a remarkable fashion the very heart of the American Fenian movement and was privy to the exact times and locations of the raids of 1870.

By this time the Dominion of Canada, now three years old, had organized the so-called Dominion Police under the direction of the aforementioned Gilbert McMicken. The Dominion Police never constituted a particularly impressive force, and by 1878 it had reached a strength of only 17 men, its main duties being to guard government buildings and protect cabinet ministers. After 1880 control passed to a commissioner of police under the federal minister of justice. By degrees the body took over responsibility for the suppression of counterfeiting and acted as an investigation bureau. It worked for the most part through local authorities or, like the U.S. treasury department, employed private detective agencies, and over time evolved into something of a Canadian counterpart to the British C.I.D., collecting police intelligence and maintaining a finger-printing bureau. But unlike the American F.B.I., the Dominion Police were a uniformed force, apart from detectives and special agents. By the end of World War I their membership totaled one hundred and fifty.

Such an essentially eastern and urban-based body was patently in no way suitable to undertake the policing portion of the vast responsibilities accepted by the Dominion when it acquired the Hudson Bay Territory in 1869. Some of the areas in question quickly began to exhibit the character of an American-style "wild west" after Hudson's Bay Company authorities relinquished supervision of the local population. Besides a small number of whites, there were some ten thousand Métis, of mixed white and Indian ancestry, and the Indians. The latter still lived under tribal government, but the need to trade for the white man's goods, including firearms, was driving them to kill off the buffalo which provided their means of livelihood, traditionally sustaining both their physical and spiritual culture. The Indians could not go on indefinitely the way they were, which became more obvious as whiskey traders based in the United States already created havoc among them.

The Canadian government at first proved scarcely more prepared than its fledgling Dominion Police Force to accept the consequences of its new northern and western territorial responsibilities, and indeed it hardly seemed to possess the resources to do so. For while Prime Minister John A. Macdonald contemplated the organization of units of mounted rifles with Royal Irish Constabulary-type duties, the Métis leader, Louis Riel, in 1869 set up a provisional government in defiance of Ottawa's authority in what is today Manitoba. Though some of Riel's opponents were imprisoned, and the provocative Ontario Orangeman Thomas Scott met his death by a provisional government firing squad under circumstances of very dubious legality, no fighting ensued when a force of Canadian militia commanded by British officers arrived from the east to expel Riel's regime. As a result the Province of Manitoba was created and joined Confederation in 1870, its lieutenant governor also having jurisdiction over the rest of the former Hudson's Bay Company lands, henceforth designated the North West Territories. Police work in Manitoba was for the most part carried out by local Canadian militia, though the province also possessed its own small force of twenty constables under Captain F. Villiers. But neither of these met the need for a force capable of patrolling the North West Territories, still the realm of the Indians. Nor did the luxury of unlimited time exist for the creation of such a force, as the whiskey traders, operating out posts like Fort Whoop Up near present day Lethbridge, Alberta, were capturing the trade in buffalo robes and demoralizing the Indians while establishing an American presence of sorts with potentially troubling implications for Canadian sovereignty.

Macdonald, the prime minister, read two reports, respectively those of Lieutenant John A. Butler of the British army and Colonel P. Robertson Rose, adjutant general of the Canadian militia, which underlined the danger of lawlessness in the territories. Balancing these reports against the expense of raising and sending a suitable police contingent west, Macdonald hesitated until the arousal of public opinion by the Cypress Hills Massacre, an event which involved the murder of a number of Indians, including women and children, by a mostly American group which included some Canadians.

The North West Mounted Police accordingly came into being at the end of August 1873, using the same ranking system as the Royal Irish Constabulary. Also like the R.I.C., constables were be expected to be literate and numerate, able to collect statistics and, in this case, customs duties. But unlike the R.I.C., the Canadian force came equipped with two field pieces, the intention being that they could if necessary fight at least limited military-type campaigns. In small arms they initially carried Adams revolvers and .577/450 calibre single shot Snider-Enfield carbines, the latter comparable to the .45-70 calibre Springfield Model 1873 carbines issued to the U.S. cavalry. This occurred at a time when repeating rifles, particularly the lever action Winchester Models 1866 and 1873, were becoming more common amongst white civilians, Métis and to some extent even Indians. Hence before many years the Canadian force realistically increased their individual and collective firepower by adopting the new Winchester Model 1876. Uniforms included the traditional British red tunic as well as blue trousers with yellow stripes, and pill-box caps for indoor and summer wear. The pill-box cap, which provided minimal protection against the elements, proved not to be a very practicable choice, being in due course replaced by more suitable headgear.

The commissioned officers initially recruited numbered nine, who came from varied backgrounds. E. Brisebois had served with the Papal Zouaves, J. Carvell was a Confederate veteran of the American Civil War, several others were ex-British army and the rest from the Canadian militia. All possessed military experience of some kind. Of other ranks above that of constable, the first man recruited was Sergeant Major A.H. Griesbach, formerly of the South African Cape Mounted Rifles, while a large component of the rest of the non-commissioned officers came from the newly founded artillery school at Kingston whose commander, George Arthur French, became the first commissioner of the force. An N.C.O. destined for future prominence was Samuel Steele, later to serve under Baden-Powell in South Africa and for a time to command the Second Canadian Division in World War I with the rank of major general. Most constables and sub-constables had seen militia service. It would have been difficult to recruit a similar force in the United States, but not impossible because of the vast numbers of Civil War veterans.

The first contingent sent to the prairies numbered one hundred and fifty and journeyed over the old fur trading route, keeping on Canadian territory. The second, of the same number, travelled through the United States by rail. During this period all telegraph communication between Manitoba and Ottawa still went via American wires, and Canadian officials and Canadian mail in transit between east and west customarily went over U.S. territory also.

Finally on the 8th of July 1874 Commissioner French had the main force ready to move west, the immediate objective being the infamous Fort Whoop Up. Unlike the Texas Rangers, they made no attempt to travel light and live partly off the land, but they were moving long distances into virtually unexplored country. The expedition consisted of two hundred and twenty-five officers and men, three hundred and ten horses, and a hundred and forty-two draught oxen. With them went twenty-three wagons and a hundred and fourteen Red River carts to carry food supplies, mowing machines, portable forges for shoeing horses, and field kitchens plus two nine-pounder field guns and two mortars. In some respects it perhaps more resembled a migration than a military expedition, but in any event trouble soon made its appearance. Horses died from exhaustion and men fell sick as they toiled in ninety degree temperatures while mosquitoes and locusts also added to the discomfort.

On the 24th of July they arrived at Roche Percee near the American frontier, having covered two hundred and twenty miles.

It was then evident that some of the force was unfit to travel west to an ill-defined destination. French thought it best to send A Division north to Fort Edmonton along a route where they could be assured of food and rest at a series of Hudson's Bay posts. On the 29th of the month French began a march west with the remaining five divisions. The food was poor and the water worse as animals died and men grew weak. By the end of August a few of the weaker horses and men were left behind where there was fresh water and sufficient grass for the animals. As their maps proved useless, French guided the party west by compass but still failed to find Fort Whoop Up. In the end necessity forced them to send men south to purchase supplies from Fort Benton in Montana, at the same time hiring guides to lead them to their intended destination.

After all this the actual arrival at Fort Whoop Up was an anti-climax as the whiskey traders, with no stomach for battle, fled. Inspector J.M. McLeod was left to establish a small post while French took the remainder of the force back east. McLeod, like all officers of the force, possessed the powers of a magistrate and consequently became the virtual governor of the far western part of the territory. His men collected customs duties and the presence of his red-coated troopers impressed the Indians. By the march across the prairies the force had already passed into legend. The legend, however, had not reached the politicians, and Commissioner French in the face of unfair attack thought it best to resign. He went on to have a distinguished career in the British army, reaching the rank of major general.

With the whisky traders expelled from the scene, the next task of the force in the west was to win the respect of, and keep the peace among, the Indians. One of the more dramatic incidents which involved them was the arrival in Canada of Sitting Bull and the Sioux after they had on the 25th of June 1876 annihilated General George Armstrong Custer and over half the U.S. 7th Cavalry on the Little Big Horn River in Montana. Sitting Bull was met by Inspector J.M. Walsh accompanied by twelve constables and three scouts. Technically a medicine man rather than a war chief but nonetheless very much a commanding figure amongst his people, the Indian leader insisted that he and the two thousand four hundred women and children and five hundred warriors who accompanied him were *Sagonash*, the Sioux word for British. He claimed that his people had been told by King George III that they would always be welcome on British territory, having been allies against the Americans in the War of 1812. Sitting Bull and his people were allowed to stay, on assurance that they would keep the peace with tribes on the Canadian side of the border. A difficulty arose, however, in the lack of enough good hunting territory for all, and after a few years' residence in Canada the band of Sioux were induced to accept an American government offer and return to the United States.

In fact the vanishing herds of buffalo made it impossible for Canadian tribes to continue their traditional way of life. In 1877, in elaborate ceremonies with a conspicuous mounted police presence, a treaty was signed whereby, in return for monetary payment, the Indians agreed to move to reservations. It then fell to the police to enforce the treaty and act as a buffer between Indians and the settlers moving onto the prairies where police posts were often the centres around which settlement grew up. Such posts also came to serve as social centres for settlers where, besides markets, dances and other festivities were held. However, serious settlement of the prairies did not get underway until the completion of the Canadian Pacific Railway in 1883. With that it became necessary to redeploy the police posts to serve the new population.

Once across the flatlands the problem was to push the rail line through the Rockies under the jurisdiction of British Columbia, which had its own police and became part of the Dominion in 1871. Nevertheless it was decided that maintenance of order among the *ad hoc* and cosmopolitan railroad construction gangs would be assigned to the Mounted Police. Sam Steele, by this time an inspector, was placed in charge in 1884. The challenge was to prevent gambling, and the sale of liquor, in a zone which extended ten miles on each side of the tracks. It was a difficult and thankless task compounded by labour troubles. In one instance Steele rose from a sick bed to read the Riot Act to striking workers who threatened to free one of their leaders held in custody.

In 1879 base pay fell from seventy-five cents a day to forty cents; those re-enlisting would receive fifty cents. A land grant of one hundred and sixty acres formerly offered to those completing a three year term of service was also withdrawn. Rations offered were poor and pay arrived irregularly. In spite of this there existed an abundance of recruits. With the advent of Commissioner A.G. Irvine in 1880 the force was brought closer to the Irish model. One part of the new arrangements was the establishment in 1883 of a training depot at Regina, Saskatchewan, which had become the real headquarters of the force. Yet Irvine's forward looking ideas were not matched by a forceful personality, and the force declined under his leadership, being at a low ebb when faced with the crisis posed by the North West Rebellion of 1885.

The Indians had continued to kill off the buffalo without mastering agricultural pursuits. As they became increasingly dependent on government rations, handed out by the Indian department which had taken over from the police, they became restless. There were a number of confrontations, as the old chiefs were losing their control of the younger warriors. While Indian discontent smouldered, the Métis, uneasy about their titles to river front land, petitioned Ottawa for reassurances. The politicians and bureaucrats chose to ignore all warnings, including those from the police.

Louis Riel again appeared on the scene, and the Métis found an able military leader in Gabriel Dumont. A trading post was seized at Duck Lake, accompanied by demands that Superintendent L.N.F. Crozier surrender the police post at Fort Carlton. Crozier at once marched on Duck Lake with fifty-six police and forty-three local militia. He was forced to retreat in the course of losing twelve men killed, twelve wounded, five horses and a seven-pounder field gun. It was evident that the revolt was too big for the Mounted Police. Some thirty-five miles away at Frog Lake, Inspector Francis Dickens, son of the novelist Charles Dickens, faced an attack by Cree Indians led by Wandering Spirit. Dickens was forced to evacuate his post called Fort Pitt. Meanwhile the Canadian volunteer militia approached from the west under Lieutenant Colonel W.D. Otter, and from the east under Major General Frederick Middleton. Otter suffered an initial check at Cut Knife Creek, but shortly after this Middleton decisively defeated the rebels at Batoche.

Only a thousand Indians out of a potential twenty thousand had actively supported the rebellion. However the Mounted Police had served as auxiliaries of the militia. They had won battle honours and like the Irish Constabulary would acquire the designation Royal. This was by no means the end of the military service in which the force was involved. Two hundred men were granted leave to fight in the Boer War. Moreover, two mounted rifle regiments sent to South Africa were commanded by former Mounties and, as noted previously, Sam Steele made a substantial contribution to the South African Constabulary. Two squadrons were sent overseas in 1916 and the Canadian military police, the Canadian Provost Corps, was organized by the Mounted Police in World War II.

Meanwhile, as the prairies filled up with settlers and the force took on more conventional police duties, a new challenge emerged in the north with the discovery of gold in the Yukon in 1896. Prospectors and miners, most of them American, began to arrive in numbers. There being no local authority in place, they set up miners' councils. An obvious danger arose that the Yukon would go the way of California. Even in Australia the two major incidences of violence, the Eureka Stockade and Lambing Flats, had arisen in the gold fields.

Inspector Charles Constantine was sent to the Arctic in 1894 for a reconaissance, returning to establish a police post the following year. There he served at one and the same time as land agent, postmaster, Indian agent, magistrate and customs officer. Like the first Mounted Police in the west, he had to communicate with Ottawa via U.S. territory. Constantine was fully established by 1896 when the Klondike rush began which led to the famous trail of '98. Constantine's original command of nineteen grew to two hundred and eighty-five. To support this force a special military contingent of two hundred was recruited. In 1898 the redoubtable Sam Steele took over from Constantine. After this a second division was established under Zachary Taylor Wood, a descendant of the American President Zachary Taylor.

Throughout the period of the trail of '98 in the Yukon, law and order on the Canadian side contrasted favourably with the conditions in neighbouring Alaska. The gold seekers had no real desire to govern themselves. They felt the need for law and order, and were content to have it provided by the police. Known criminals could be kept out because the police controlled the entrance to, and exit from, the gold field. Apart from this many lives were saved as the police insisted that those using the dangerous waterways of the Yukon travelled in safe boats under the direction of experienced navigators. As prices were high, Steele insisted that everyone entering the territory must possess either two months' provisions and $500, or six months' provisions and $200. The entire Yukon service of the police was essentially crime prevention, the kind of duty which is so often ignored and so rarely recognized. The disorders in California and in Alaska were romantic but unnecessary: a Mounted Police-style organization could have ensured law and order.

After the turn of the century it seemed that the Royal North West Mounted Police were but an aspect of a fast-vanishing frontier. As each province organized its own police, the R.N.W.M.P. would retreat to the Arctic and become a small force relegated to vast but largely uninhabited federal territories. Manitoba and British Columbia had their own provincial police. In 1905 when Alberta and Saskatchewan became provinces, it was agreed that the R.N.W.M.P. would continue for the time-being. This took the form of a five-year contract. In return for $25,000 each province would be served by two hundred and fifty R.N.W.M.P. who would act under the provincial attorney general. At this time the annual cost of the force was about $1,000,000. Their contract was renewed in 1911, but as the Mounted Police were thin on the ground and unable to control the rising crime rate, there seemed to be a strong case for the organization of provincial forces by the time of the outbreak of World War I.

The first thought of many Mounties in 1914 was to enlist in the Canadian Expeditionary Force, but their services at home remained indispensable. They faced the vast problem of the surveillance of some two hundred thousand enemy aliens in Alberta and Saskatchewan among recent immigrants from central Europe, and of patrolling the border of the neutral United States which was an obvious base from which enemy agents could operate. The force accordingly expanded from five hundred to twelve hundred men, but there was nothing like the war hysteria which characterized the American entrance into the conflict three years later. Nonetheless, the police did find themselves plagued by self-appointed and self-important investigators who suffered from spy fever. Dangerous aliens were few and busybodies with their misdirected if usually well-intentioned activities were by the same token soon brought under control. Rumours of cross-border raids in 1916 led Ottawa to insist on the withdrawal of the Mounties from regular civil policing. Provincial police, who were already in existence in Saskatchewan and Manitoba, took over all provincial duties in June 1917 and in Alberta did the same in March 1918.

Yet with the U.S. declaration of war on the Central Powers in April 1917, the threat of border raids vanished. It then looked as though the R.N.W.M.P. had had their day. In April 1918 seven hundred and sixty men went overseas. In August another hundred and eighty-four were sent to Siberia as part of a larger Canadian force during the Russian Civil War. By the end of World War I only a skeleton force of three hundred and three men remained in Canada. Ottawa decided to keep the force as a federal police in the west to complement the Dominion Police serving in the east. Thus the force was assured of a permanent existence and recruited up to twelve hundred. At the time a constable was raised from $1.25 a day to $1.75 and men overseas were returned to Canada.

The year was 1919 and Canadians were affected by the "Red scare" which swept the continent. As there was no bombing and no vigilante tradition in Canada, the Canadian reaction was milder. There existed, nevertheless, considerable social unrest combined with revolutionary literature circulated by those sympathetic to the new Soviet regime in Russia. The R.N.W.M.P. was assigned the task of infiltrating subversive organizations in the interests of internal security. It was also in the interest of the groups themselves, as indicated by the case of Michael Murphy and the Toronto Fenians. Unfortunately the Mounted Police were not the only source of information and the Winnipeg general strike so alarmed some of the middle class in the city that they manifested a tendency toward vigilantism through the organization of a citizens' committee. Between twenty and thirty thousand workers were on strike. Difficulties arose when the strike committee gave orders to permit essential services to operate. This was in the public interest, but was seen as an assumption of police power. Matters were further complicated when the police who were themselves unionized were ordered to sign an agreement not to strike under any circumstances. Their refusal led to the citizens' committee insisting on the hiring of special constables who attempted to take over police work. When these amateurs bungled the job badly, they became objects of ridicule and abuse.

Meanwhile the strike leaders were in some degree dependent on convinced revolutionaries for the leg work involved in organizing a strike. The price they had to pay for this was the tolerance of revolutionary literature and posters which gave the citizens' committee cause for alarm. Meanwhile reports of secret agents cautioned that the leaders of the strike committee had no plans for escalating the strike into a revolution. Commissioner A.B. Perry gave assurances to the cabinet ministers that revolution was not on the agenda. If they had acted on this information, the ensuing violence might have been avoided. There were, however, other sources of information. The American Secret Service had been watching the Soviet agent Ludwig Martens, mentioned in the previous chapter. They reported that Martens had sent money to Canada to found a radical publication fund. The Canadian who received the money — about $7,000 — gave it to the strike committee. At the same time it is possible that British intelligence had correctly reported that the Soviets were sending money to North America. It is difficult to determine how much this information influenced the decision of Minister of Justice Gideon Robertson to arrest the strike committee. As he came to Winnipeg to investigate he must in some degree have been influenced by the prevailing fear of violence among the leading citizens of Winnipeg. Having arrested the strike committee, he beheaded a movement which was already defeated and left control of the workers in the hands of second line leaders. These were unable or perhaps unwilling to restrain tendencies toward violence.

When a demonstration for the release of the leaders was ordered, the mayor of Winnipeg, Charles Gray, forbade it but could not prevent a parade down Main Street in defiance of the ban. It was obvious that the special constables could not hope to control the gathering crowds. There followed an incident which has gone down in left-wing folk lore as "Bloody Saturday." The ignoring of police intelligence reports by the government left the Mounted Police the responsibility of facing violence that need never have arisen. As the militia, which in other circumstances might have been called out, was deemed incapable of effective action, some fifty Mounted Police on horseback supported by another thirty-six in trucks were sent out to control a crowd estimated as high as fifteen thousand. The Riot Act had been read without effect and the police were attacked by missiles of various kinds, wounding horses and men. The police rode through the mob twice in efforts to displace them. Having failed to do so the police fired on the crowd, killing one and wounding another twenty-four. Six constables were injured.

The strike was lost, but labour historians gained a legend, which in the version of the extreme left became a story of police brutality. In the more immediate sense Ottawa was pleased with the performance of the R.N.W.M.P. and alarmed by the sympathy with the strikers displayed by the Winnipeg Municipal Police. It was decided that a national force was needed. The force was expanded to two thousand five hundred men, merged with the small Dominion Police, and given jurisdiction across Canada. The Royal North West Mounted Police became in 1920 the Royal Canadian Mounted Police. Four new divisions were established and headquarters moved from Regina to Ottawa. Secret service work would be continued, and cover all of the Dominion. At this time it was merely a federal police with full responsibility in the north west. In 1928 it resumed provincial policing in Saskatchewan; in 1932 it took over all remaining provincial responsibilities in all provinces save Quebec, Ontario and British Columbia.

The primary cause was economy. It was a depression year and the R.C.M.P.'s services were cheaper than an independent provincial force. British Columbia had organized an R.I.C.-style

A Royal Canadian Mounted Policeman, seen here flanked by members of the Metropolitan Toronto Mounted Unit, taking part in the Queen's Birthday Parade, Toronto, 1995. (Photo: Ken Tollis).

police in 1858, and did not accept the R.C.M.P. as provincial police until 1950. Newfoundland had organized an R.I.C.-type police in 1870 which survives as the municipal police of the city of St. John's. Provincial policing was assigned to the Newfoundland Rangers in 1935, who were absorbed by the R.C.M.P. in 1949, a year after Newfoundland joined Confederation. Ontario Provincial Police were organized in 1909 and remain a less romantic but nevertheless effective police to the present day. The present Quebec Provincial Police were organized in 1870 and, because of the strength of provincial nationalism, there could be no question of the province transferring this police power to a federal agency. The R.C.M.P. in the province is kept busy enforcing federal laws.

The R.C.M.P., like the London Metropolitan Police, is among the most famous of the world's police forces. The combination of the red coat and the west captured the public imagination from the beginning. The Mounties, however, have carefully nourished their own legend. The musical ride which is now the only mounted service performed by the corps apart from ceremonial escort duties, owes its origin to a display of riding given as early as 1876. Today it has acquired an international reputation, appearing in New York's Madison Square Garden for the first time in 1939. The first film about the Mounties was made in 1910 and films about the force reached a climax with the production of the Hollywood musical *Rose Marie*, starring Jeanette Macdonald and Nelson Eddy in 1936. It is probably the most popular film ever made about Canada, although Canadians had little to do with it.

By degrees the R.C.M.P. took over and combined functions performed in the United States by the F.B.I. and state troopers. It remains today, in spite of clamour in the press and a body of anti-police literature, one of the most popular police forces in the world, and so it is likely to remain for some time to come.

CHAPTER XI

CONCLUSIONS

OLICE WORK IS A CONSEQUENCE of the division of labour in maturing civilization. In its Commonwealth and American context the emergence of professional police was long and unnecessarily delayed because of the fear of state action of any kind. These fears were not without foundation as police power can so easily be made to serve the interest of those holding political power. On the European Continent the modern bureaucratic state was built on the ashes of mediaeval constitutionalism. Efforts to correct this by revolution as in the case of Jacobin France merely brought out the worst, most ruthless features of police power. In the Anglo-American and Commonwealth experience, a much modified mediaeval constitutional tradition ante-dated the growth of the bureaucratic state. The Revolutions of 1688 and 1776 had very little effect on local government. The Cromwellian interlude was in the nature of an internal conquest by which an extreme Puritan minority dominated society without much popular support. The only effect it had was to strengthen the already powerful inclination to resist state power. The police work of the Continental Congress and its supporters had the character of vigilantism which was already a visible aspect of American society in colonial times. The resistance to crown forces during the revolution rarely involved the use of state power.

The success of early efforts to introduce professional police owes more to the ideas of the Radical Utilitarians than to the desire of the privileged classes to protect property. The London Metropolitan Police survived, and later flourished, on its merits, but it profited by the support of individual Radicals like Francis Place. New York policing was a mere generation behind its London model, but suffered from the continued influence of political patronage which in America remained at the eighteenth century level almost to the present day. Professionalism in any form long remained suspect as an alien monarchical innovation. The lingering of obvious partisan political affiliation did much to deprive municipal police in the United States of the public confidence which the London police enjoyed.

Montreal leaned heavily on the garrison of British regulars in the city until the Gavarazzi Riot of 1853. In any case a large section of the police were drawn from former soldiers as were most of their senior officers during the first half of the nineteenth century. As time went on, however, Montreal police became more like American police but on the whole had a better grip on crime than their American counterparts who admittedly faced far larger problems. Outside Montreal, in the period immediately after the Rebelllion of 1837, Quebec police not only drew upon the services of former soldiers, but alumnae of the Irish County Constabulary. Although the Montreal force began as unarmed police, like the New York police they had to acquire arms in the face of an armed underworld.

The London Metropolitan Police proved to be an adequate model for rural Britain and most Irish cities. Yet there was never a question of their type of police being effective in rural Ireland where landlord-tenant conflict and Protestant-Catholic tension gave rise to partly armed secret societies with no respect for the moral authority of the law. During the protracted period of the French wars of 1793-1815, which included the Irish Rebellion of 1798, the policing of rural Ireland was carried out by the military under magistrates given exceptional powers under a series of temporary Insurrection Acts. As this system could not survive the post-war demobilization of most of the army, Robert Peel sought to meet the new challenge through the creation of the Peace Preservation

Force, which today would be called a "S.W.A.T." squad. It could not prevent crime by patrol or control the kind of widespread disturbances which often swept the country. Moreover the Peace Preservation Force was opposed by the unpaid local magistrates because when it was employed all justices of the peace acted under the authority and direction of a Castle-appointed stipendiary magistrate. By the same token the county at first met all, and then part, of the cost of this special corps.

The limitations of Peel's force led to the creation of the County Constabulary in 1822, which was acceptable to the magistrates because they made the appointments to the body at the local level. The organization of the County Constabulary coincided with the emergence of Daniel O'Connell's Catholic Association. This popular movement, which activated large sections of the general public, took the initiative away from the secret societies, but did not altogether displace them. O'Connell undoubtedly benefitted from the existence of the County Constabulary although he could not admit it. They in turn found a legal, constitutional mass movement less formidable or at least less physically threatening than violent, illegal secret societies. The best evidence of this is the fact that the Constabulary lost control of the Irish countryside when success dissolved the Catholic Association.

Between 1829 and 1835 such a breakdown of law and order occurred that the government was forced to re-activate the Orange- dominated volunteer militia, the Yeomanry, thus in effect arming one section of the population against the other. Not until 1835 was Irish Under-Secretary Thomas Drummond able to create the force which won the respect if not the praise of the Irish. Drummond organized an armed, uniformed barrack police which by degrees became a predominately Catholic force reflecting the religion of the majority. Appointments were made by the crown and the new constabulary undertook such mundane civic responsibilities as the collection of statistics. It was this force which became the model for colonial police throughout the empire and commonwealth. It was impossible to re-create an entirely faithful copy yet, while adjustments to local cultural and other conditions were necessary, the imitation was nevertheless conscious and deliberate.

India presented the greatest overseas police challenge but the problem did not become acute until the first quarter of the nineteenth century. Historic Indian police arrangements no longer functioned and Britain had yet to develop a professional police of its own. The *darogha* system filled the gap but ran counter to the spirit of bureaucratic reform inspired by the Utilitarians. As the army was doing more than its share of police work, it is not surprising that a soldier-intellectual in the person of Sir Charles Napier conceived the idea of an R.I.C.-style police for India. It was first adopted in the newly acquired Sind, and by 1862 with modifications was introduced throughout India. The force which was finally organized was neither purely military like Napier's force nor an exact copy of the R.I.C. There would be literate unarmed police who collected statistics and enforced the law. These would be supported by an often illiterate armed police who would act as security guards. The officer corps was until the turn of the century, with very few exceptions, European; and it remained in senior ranks predominately European until the eve of independence. Like the R.I.C. it was never a popular force, but the best testimony to its effectiveness is its survival under post-independence governments.

Australia was settled on the eve of major bureaucratic reform in Britain, and there was as yet no model for the new settlements to adopt. There was need to use some of the more reliable convicts as constables even while retaining heavy dependence on the military. The emergence of the bush rangers, a body of formidable if romantic outlaws, and disorder in the gold fields at the Eureka Stockade and Lambing Flats, point to the inadequacies of these early police arrangements. The London model would after a fashion be useful in the cities, but for rural policing the R.I.C. was the thing. The scattered nature of the settlements made policing by individual constables essential, hence the need for a carefully selected, well trained and amply paid force. After 1862 these needs were met by producing a series of forces, each based on a single colony, which were among the most effective in the world. Native trackers were incorporated into these organizations, and camels successfully employed in the torrid heat of the inland deserts.

In South Africa all forces were and had to be mixed forces, because the population was predominately black. The Cape Mounted Rifles, which ante-date the founding of the R.I.C., owe little to the Irish model; they were essentially frontier police whose task but not organization paralleled the Texas Rangers. The Natal Mounted Police were modelled on the Cape Mounted Rifles, being a mixed force, and recruiting partly in Britain. Yet they were more than a frontier force, as they had to patrol the entire province. The Natal Police consequently bore greater resemblance to the R.I.C. while different from them as they were equipped for, and often engaged in, actual warfare. Baden-Powell's South African Constabulary was unique in Africa and unique in history, conceived and created by his remarkable personality. It was recruited from all the white parts of the empire while, like the other African police, including a large native contingent. After a creditable performance in the Boer War it undertook its original task of patrolling the territory of the former Boer republics. It shares with the London Metropolitan Police and the R.N.W.M.P. the characteristic of winning the confidence of those it was supposed to protect.

The American colonies, first settled in the seventeenth century, grew up with English mediaeval police institutions. They were never adequate to police frontier areas, hence the field was left open for the emergence of self-policing which took the name of vigilantism. The vigilantes were a mixed lot, in some cases organized in secret societies as night riders, in others functioning publicly as in California under the leadership of a journalist. The only formal police were the Texas Rangers, who passed into folklore and became internationally famous. They started as frontier police and toward the end of the century evolved into state police. As a highly competent and relatively inexpensive frontier police they were unsurpassed, but they were too much children of the frontier. Like many frontiersmen they collected Indian scalps, and during the Mexican War they were with good reason suspected of taking no prisoners.

The sheriff and marshal as police officers produced some remarkable individuals like Wyatt Earp, but as folklore clearly demonstrates, they were also aspects of the wild west. As local officials they could not protect goods in transit, particularly those travelling by rail. Such protection was provided by private agencies, particularly the company organized as a private detective agency by Alan Pinkerton which filled to some extent the gap long left by the absence of federal police. The agents of the Pinkerton Detective Agency rivalled the exploits of the more famous sheriffs and marshals. Pinkerton, being originally in turn a Scottish Chartist and an American abolitionist, at first sought to avoid labour disputes. His agency became involved in them by its successful efforts to end the terrorism of the Molly Maguires in the Pennsylvania coal fields. After that the Pinkertons became a *bête noire* of labour historians but continued as a conventional private protection agency. After an amateurish beginning the Federal Bureau of Investigation became professional under the direction of J. Edgar Hoover. It was certainly a popular force in the 1930s because of its attacks on organized crime. In the post-World War II era it fell under attack by the left because of Hoover's efforts to deal with Communist influence, but the F.B.I. retained the confidence of more conservative Americans.

The Hudson's Bay Company territories acquired by the new Dominion of Canada in 1867 were in danger of turning into an American-style wild west, and would most certainly have done so had the North West Mounted Police not marched to the foothills of the Rockies in 1874. This force bore some resemblance to the Cape Mounted Rifles of South Africa in that it was at first equipped with artillery and prepared to fight small wars. It was however more in the spirit of the R.I.C. which contributed many men to its ranks. It marched into folklore as it went west in 1874 and consequently never suffered from a lack of recruits. It was in spite of its reputation an under-paid and much neglected organization whose commander possessed very little political influence. A close examination of its records, particularly by hostile witnesses, revealed many faults. Yet taking the long view, its achievements stand. It put an end to whiskey trading, moved the Indians to reservations without Indian wars, kept the peace in the Yukon gold fields, and provided accurate if neglected intelligence at the time of the Winnipeg general strike. After it became a force with national responsibilities it was able to provide most provinces with less expensive police service than they could have provided from their own resources.

All American and Commonwealth forces had to operate under common law. From the police point of view this constituted a handicap, although it afforded the public protection against the abuse of police power. The absence of what is called "absolutism" in Anglo-American history reflects a sense of the rule of law and due process which was recognized in the oaths taken by Saxon kings and underlined in the *Magna Carta*. This sense of lawful government unnecessarily retarded the development of profession al police. Part of the price was a lawless London in the eighteenth century and the American wild west in the nineteenth. Yet the price having been paid, the result was a series of police forces which were clearly under civil authority. This would not be much of an advantage when the civil authority itself was corrupt, but the latter condition could be corrected by the democratic process.

The models for nearly all Anglo-American and Commonwealth forces were the London Metropolitan Police and the Royal Irish Constabulary. The American west is an exception to this, but as the work of trooper police in Australia and Canada demonstrates, the exception could have been avoided. The state troopers in the various American states are not conscious imitations of the R.I.C., but they embody many of the same features. In one case at least, that of the New Jersey State Troopers, there was some help offered early in the century by R.N.W.M.P. personnel.

Policing is an unpleasant aspect of life which in a stable society requires little attention. In complex societies subject to the pressures of change, policing cannot be safely neglected. It is best placed in the hands of professionals, and the history of the Commonwealth and United States is the story of efforts, for the most part successful, in keeping professionals under the law.

BIBLIOGRAPHY

INTRODUCTION TO THE BIBLIOGRAPHY

HILE THERE EXISTS A VAST body of literature dealing with the police history of common law jurisdictions, the more important and more readable items are included in the following bibliography. An excellent general introduction to the British aspect of police is Charles Reith, *A New Study of Police History*. John Coatman's *Police* also provides a useful overview while, of several other surveys, George Howard's *Guardians of the Queen's Peace* is among the best. For those wanting a detailed study of English mediaeval police arrangements, the F.W. Maitland classic published in 1885, *Justice and Police*, remains a must. For the age of the Fielding brothers, Patrick Pringle's *Hue and Cry* is the most readable. The Rowan and Mayne period is effectively covered by the Reith study mentioned above. James F. Richardson, *The New York Police: Colonial Times to 1901*, is comprehensive and sound, but Joel Tyler Headley's vintage *The Great Riots of New York, 1712 to 1873* provides more colour. My wife, Elinor Kyte Senior, offers a window into Montreal police history in her article, "The Influence of the British Garrison on the Development of the Montreal Police, 1832 to 1853," published in the April 1979 issue of *Military Affairs*.

Galen Broeker, *Rural Disorder and Police Reform in Ireland, 1812-1836*, provides the background for the events which led to the founding of what became the Royal Irish Constabulary. For a detailed account of the earlier period of Irish police, there is S.H. Palmer, *Police and Protest in England and Ireland, 1750-1850*. Richard Bennett, *The Black and Tans*, provides a vivid but balanced account of the controversial last days of the Royal Irish Constabulary.

There are many works on Indian police, including recent sociological studies and memoir material by former police officials. Prabhu Sharma, *Indian Police: A Developmental Approach*, is a very able study, but for a general picture J.C. Curry's *Indian Police*, published in 1932, offers the best introduction. D. Chappell and P.R. Wilson, *The Police and the Public in Australia and New Zealand*, provides a competent survey, but A.L. Haydon's *Trooper Police of Australia*, an older study, conveys more of the flavour of Australian policing. There is still much to be written about South African police. T.J. Van Heerden's *Introduction to Police Science* includes a brief historical survey. Lord Baden-

Powell, *Lessons from the 'Varsity of Life*, provides a chapter on his unique adventure in policing; and H.P. Holt, *The Mounted Police of Natal*, is something of a South African counterpart to Haydon's record of Australian police work.

By far the best account of the American "wild west" is Wayne Gard's *Frontier Justice*, while Frank Shay, *Judge Lynch: His First Hundred Years*, also deals with eastern and southern aspects of lynch law. Walter Prescott Webb, *The Texas Rangers: A Century of Frontier Defense*, remains the most authoritative, and an invaluable, study of that famous body; but Stephen Hardin, *The Texas Rangers*, a more recent production, concisely carries the Ranger story more nearly to the present day. James D. Horan, *The Pinkertons: The Detective Dynasty that Made History*, is a good, sound piece of work. Among the considerable quantity of literature dealing with the R.C.M.P. and its N.W.M.P. predecessor, S.W. Horrall's *Pictorial History of the Royal Canadian Mounted Police* serves as an able introduction. More detail can be found in Nora and William Kelly, *The Royal Canadian Mounted Police: A Century of History, 1873-1973*, though Samuel B. Steele's *Forty Years in Canada* should also be read by all with a serious interest in the force. For those concerned with labour history, SW. Horrall, "The Royal North-West Mounted Police and Labour Unrest in Western Canada, 1919," in the *Canadian Historical Review* (1980), throws new light on the role of the Mounties in the Winnipeg General Strike, particularly.

Baden-Powell, Lord. *Lessons from the 'Varsity of Life*. London: C. Arthur Pearson Ltd., 1933.

Bayley, David H. *The Police and Political Development in India*. Princeton: Princeton University Press, 1969.

Bennett, Richard. *The Black and Tans*. rev. ed., London: Severn House Publishers Ltd., 1976.

Broehl, Wayne G. *The Molly Maguires*. Cambridge: Harvard University Press, 1964.

Broeker, Galen. *Rural Disorder and Police Reform in Ireland, 1812-1836*. London: Routledge and Kegan Paul, 1970.

Bruce, William Napier. *The Life of General Sir Charles Napier, G.C.B.*. London: John Murray, 1885.

Brunell, Jacques and Pierre. *The Royal Canadian Mounted Police in the 1990s: Their Uniforms and Kit*. Winnipeg: Bunker to Bunker Books, 1994.

Chappell, D. and P.R. Wilson. *The Police and the Public in Australia and New Zealand*. St. Lucia: University of Queensland Press, 1969.

Coakley, Leo J. *Jersey Troopers: A Fifty Year History of the New Jersey State Police*. New Brunswick, N.J.: Rutgers University Press, 1971.

Coatman, John. *Police*. London: Oxford University Press, 1959.

Cobb, Belton. *The First Detectives and the Early Career of Richard Mayne, Commissioner of Police*. London: Faber and Faber, 1957.

Cox, Sir Edmund C. *Police and Crime in India*. London: Stanley Paul and Co., n.d.

Critchley, T.A. *A History of Police in England and Wales, 900- 1966*. London: Constable, 1967.

Cross, Wilbur L. *The History of Henry Fielding*. New York: Russell and Russell, 1963.

Curry, J.C. *Indian Police*. London: Faber and Faber, 1932.

Cutler, James Elbert. *Lynch-Law: An Investigation into the History of Lynching in the United States*. Montclair, N.J.: Patterson Smith, 1969.

Ex C.M.R. *With the Cape Mounted Rifles: Four Years Service in South Africa*. London: Richard Bentley and Son, 1881.

Fox, Arthur. *The Newfoundland Constabulary*. St. John's: Robinson Blackmore Ltd., 1971.

Gard, Wayne. *Frontier Justice*. Norman: University of Oklahoma Press, 1949.

Gillett, James B. *Six Years with the Texas Rangers, 1875 to 1881* ed. Milo Milton Quaife. Chicago: The Lakeside Press, 1943.

Goldring, Philip. *The First Contingent: The North-West Mounted Police, 1873-74*. Ottawa: National Historic Parks and Sites Branch, 1979.

Crabb, Cyril *Queensland Desperadoes: Wild Tales of Bushranging Days*. London and Sydney: Angus and Robertson Publishers, 1983.

Greer, Allan. "The Birth of the Police in Canada," in Allan Greer and Ian Radforth, eds., *Colonial Leviathan: State Formation in Mid-Nineteenth-Century Canada*, Toronto: University of Toronto Press, 1992.

Hardin, Stephen. *The Texas Rangers*. London: Osprey Publishing Ltd, 1991.

Hart, J.M. *The British Police*. London: Allen and Unwin, 1951.

Haydon, A.L. *The Trooper Police of Australia: A Record of Mounted Police Work in the Commonwealth from the Earliest Days of Settlement to the Present Time*. London: Andrew Melrose, 1911.

Headley, Joel Tyler. *The Great Riots of New York, 1712 to 1873; Including a Full and Complete Account of the Four Days' Draft Riot of 1863*. New York: Dover Publications, 1971.

Holt, H.P. *The Mounted Police of Natal*. London: John Murray, 1913.

Horan, James D. *The Pinkertons: The Detective Dynasty that Made History*. New York: Crown Publishers, Inc., 1967.

Horrall, S.W. *Pictorial History of the Royal Canadian Mounted Police*. Toronto: McGraw Hill-Ryerson, 1973.

Horrall, S.W. "The Royal North-West Mounted Police and Labour Unrest in Western Canada, 1919," *Canadian Historical Review*, LXI, 2, 1980.

Horwood, Harold. *A History of the Newfoundland Ranger Force*. St. John's: Breakwater Books Ltd., 1986.

Howard, George. *Guardians of the Queen's Peace: The Development and Work of Britain's Police*. London: Odhams Press Ltd., 1953.

Howe, Sir Ronald. *The Story of Scotland Yard: A History of the C.I.D. from the Earliest Times to the Present Day*. London: A. Barker, 1965.

Idriess, Ion L. *Man Tracks: With the Mounted Police in Australian Wilds*. Sydney: Angus and Robertson Ltd., 1935.

Kelly, Nora and William. *The Royal Canadian Mounted Police: A Century of History, 1873-1973*. Edmonton: Hurtig Publishers, 1973.

Kennedy, Edward B. *The Black Police of Queensland: Reminiscences of Official Work and Personal Adventures in the Early Days of the Colony*. London: John Murray, 1902.

Lucas, T.J. *Camp Life and Sport in South Africa: Experiences of Kaffir Warfare with the Cape Mounted Rifles*. Johannesburg: Africana Book Society, 1975.

Lucas, Thomas J. *The Zulus and the British Frontiers*. New York: Negro Universities Press, 1969.

Macbeth, R.G. *Policing the Plains: Being the Real-Life Record of the Famous Royal North-West Mounted Police*. London: Hodder and Stoughton, 1921.

Macleod, R.C. *The North West Mounted Police, 1873-1919*. Ottawa: Canadian Historical Association, 1978.

Maitland, Frederic William. *Justice and Police*. London: Macmillan, 1885.

Marquis, Greg. *Policing Canada's Century: A History of the Canadian Association of Chiefs of Police*. Toronto: The Osgoode Society, 1993.

Palmer, S.H. *Police and Protest in England and Ireland, 1780-1850*. Cambridge and New York: Cambridge University Press, 1988.

Pringle, Patrick. *Hue and Cry: The Birth of the British Police*. London: Museum Press, 1955.

Reith, Charles. *The Blind Eye of History: A Study of the Origin of the Present Police Era*. Montclair, N.J.: Patterson Smith, 1975.

Reith, Charles. *A New Study of Police History*. Edinburgh and London: Oliver and Boyd, 1956.

Reynolds, E.E. *Baden-Powell: A Biography of Lord Baden-Powell of Gilwell*. London and New York: Oxford University Press, 1943.

Reynolds, Paul Kenneth Baillie. *The Vigiles of Imperial Rome*. London: Oxford University Press, 1926.

Richardson, James F. *The New York Police: Colonial Times to 1901*. New York: Oxford University Press, 1970.

Saha, B.P. *Indian Police: Legacy and Quest for Formative Role*. Delhi: Konark PVT Publishers Ltd., 1990.

Senior, Elinor Kyte. "The Influence of the British Garrison on the Development of the Montreal Police, 1832 to 1853," *Military Affairs*, XLIII, April 1979.

Sharma, Prabhu Datta. *Indian Police: A Developmental Approach*. New Delhi: Research Publications in Social Sciences, 1977.

Shay, Frank. *Judge Lynch: His First Hundred Years*. Montclair, N.J.: Patterson Smith, 1969.

Smith, Bruce. *Police Systems in the United States*. New York and London: Harper and Brothers Publishers, 1940.

Steele, Samuel B. *Forty Years in Canada: Reminiscences of the Great North-West with Some Account of His Service in South Africa*, Toronto: McGraw-Hill Ryerson Ltd., 1972.

Stewart, Robert. *Sam Steele: Lion of the Frontier*. Toronto and Garden City, N.Y.: Doubleday and Co., 1979.

Thomson, Basil. *The Story of Scotland Yard*. Garden City, N.J.: Doubleday, Doran and Company, 1936.

Trivedi, S.D. *Secret Services in Ancient India: Techniques and Operations*. New Delhi and Bombay: Allied Publishers Private Ltd., 1984.

Van Heerden, T.J. *Introduction to Police Science*. Pretoria: University of South Africa Press, 1982.

Watters, Pat and Stephen Gillers. *Investigating the FBI*. Garden City, N.Y.: Doubleday and Co., Inc., 1973.

Webb, Walter Prescott. *The Texas Rangers: A Century of Frontier Defense*. Austin: University of Texas Press, 1991.

Whitehead, Don. *The FBI Story: A Report to the People*. New York: Random House, 1956.

Williams, Robert Hamilton. *With the Border Ruffians: Memories of the Far West, 1852-1868*. ed. E.W. Williams, Toronto: Musson Book Co. Ltd., 1919.

Woodruff, Philip. *The Men Who Ruled India: The Founders*. London: Jonathan Cape, 1965.

Woodruff, Philip. *The Men Who Ruled India: The Guardians*. London: Jonathan Cape, 1965.

Wynne, Martin, ed. *On Honourable Terms: The Memoirs of Some Indian Police Officers, 1915-1948*. London: Bacsa, 1985.

INDEX